F*CK WHALES

ALSO FAMILIES, POETRY, FOLKSY WISDOM AND YOU

Petty Essays from a Brilliant Mind

MADDOX

Illustrations by Jessica Safron
and Louis Fernet-Leclair

GALLERY BOOKS
New York London Sydney Toronto New Delhi

G

Gallery Books
An Imprint of Simon & Schuster, Inc.
1230 Avenue of the Americas
New York, NY 10020

Copyright © 2017 by Maddox

Image credits on page 245.

Certain names and identifying characteristics have been changed, whether or not
so noted in the text.

First Gallery Books hardcover edition October 2017

GALLERY BOOKS and colophon are registered trademarks of
Simon & Schuster, Inc.

For information about special discounts for bulk purchases, please contact Simon
& Schuster Special Sales at 1-866-506-1949 or business@simonandschuster.com.

The Simon & Schuster Speakers Bureau can bring authors to your live event. For
more information or to book an event, contact the Simon & Schuster Speakers
Bureau at 1-866-248-3049 or visit our website at www.simonspeakers.com.

Interior design by Jaime Putorti

Manufactured in the United States of America

10 9 8 7 6 5 4 3 2 1

Library of Congress Cataloging-in-Publication Data is available.

ISBN 978-1-4767-9497-6
ISBN 978-1-4767-9498-3 (ebook)

First, fuck dedications.

Second, this is for the same person I dedicated my first book to.
You mean the world to me.
I love you.

CONTENTS

Fuck Whales   1

Fuck Tables   9

Fuck Horses   13

Fuck Trees   23

Fuck Families   29

Fuck Cupcakes   33

Fuck Folksy Wisdom   37

Fuck Silhouette Photos   43

Fuck Fictional Serials   45

Fuck Poetry   49

Fuck Your Weight-Loss Insecurity   55

Fuck Children (but Don't)   57

Fuck Online Reviews   61

Fuck Dichotomies   67

Fuck Dog Lovers   71

Fuck Your Objection to Sexual Objectification   77

Fuck Your Shitty Opinions   85

Fuck Being Offended   91

Fuck Abstraction   101

Fuck Your Racist Witch Hunt   107

Fuck Being Proud of Who You Are   113

Fuck Following Your Dreams   115

Fuck Censorship   119

Fuck Bodies   123

Fuck the Approval of Your Loved Ones   127

Fuck Old Ideas   131

Fuck Raising Awareness   135

Fuck Being Cold   143

Fuck Feigned Sympathy   145

Fuck People Who Want to Get Rid of Jerks   147

Fuck Vegetarians Who Won't Eat Leftover Meat   151

Fuck Your Arbitrary Sympathy Complex   155

Fuck Stupid Relationship Questions   161

Fuck Hard Decisions   165

Fuck CAPTCHAs   167

Fuck Environmentalists   171

Fuck Baby Talk   175

Fuck Parents Who Don't Want My Parenting Advice   179

Fuck the Eighth Amendment   183

Fuck Soulmates   189

Fuck People Who Are Afraid of Lightning and Thunder   195

Fuck Trigger Warnings   197

Fuck People Who Agree with You   207

Fuck Maternity and Paternity Leave   213

Fuck Rhymes   217

Fuck Ants   221

Fuck Your Opinion on Humanity   225

Fuck You   229

Acknowledgments   235

Notes   239

Illustration Credits   245

FUCK WHALES

No other animal gets as much of a free pass as whales do, and no other animal deserves it less. What has a whale ever done for you? That's not a rhetorical question. Think about your first day of school, or when you learned to tie your shoelaces, or the long summer you worked to earn your first car, or applying to college, or having a child. Everything you've ever done, from folding loads of laundry to locking your door when you go to sleep at night, was done without the aid of a whale. These pale gray abominations—and they are gray, let's not kid ourselves with fairy tales about them being blue—have never done anything for you or anyone you care about.

Whales Suck at Everything, Including Death

If a whale fulfills its lot in life, it will likely end up on a beach, where it will spend its time rotting under the sun, emanating a waft of pungent sea-funk that will serve only to ruin beach outings for months to come (Fig. 1).

Removing the whale carcass presents a unique challenge because the job requires a complete disregard for one's own happiness and olfactory health. The most useful outcome for a dead

Fig. 1: Here's a fat, stupid, idiot whale ruining everyone's day at the beach by dying all over it. Fuck you, whale.

whale should be to end up on our plates, but whales even suck at being food. The mercury levels in whale meat can exceed the recommended limit by 200 times.[1] That means if you're pregnant—and I assume you are, until I know otherwise—simply doing your part to dispose of a dead whale, by eating it, will give your child birth defects. That brain damage, in a roundabout way, could be the only positive thing that can be said about whales. It could potentially employ a neurosurgeon.

Yet in spite of their complete lack of contributions to humanity, they get from us an undue amount of respect and compassion. Whales are the charity cases of the sea. They subsist equally on krill and empathy from idiots (Fig. 2).

Whales are always in need of saving. No other being, except for the queen of England, has ever needed so much saving as a whale. At least with the queen, it's up to God to save her, as opposed to us. It's like the ocean is one giant level of Super Mario Brothers, and the princess is 150 tons of blubber. Every time you save one whale, it proceeds to have offspring that also

Fig. 2: Just another unemployed bum begging for scraps. Get a job!

need saving. It's like trying to save a cat from a burning house while it gives birth to a litter of kittens that all run around the burning house. There's no way to help whales, except with a harpoon. However, that's a waste of steel. In an ideal world, people would be more concerned about saving the harpoons. Harpoons have uses; whales do not.

Whales Are Drinking All Our Water and Eating Our Sailors

Whales are drinking our water, but they're not even good at doing that, because there's still some left. They need to drink all the oceans dry, so every last whale is beached on a desert of his own creation. When whales aren't eating our sailors, which is never, they're luring them into blasphemous, lifelong obsessions.

Years ago, I wrote a celebrated article titled "When Was the Last Time a Whale Did Anything for You?" Over the years, this essay has elicited much angry hate mail from whale apologists. Here's one such exchange:

From: Ashley
Subject: Think again!
You know NOTHING about whales. Whales are loving creatures! They DO NOT eat people! Nor do they drink water other than when they suck in water to feed on krill. Did I mention a killer whale has NEVER hurt anybody in the wild? The only thing to blame is humans. They slaughter them, and put killer whales in captivity! Whales go mad in captivity! Next time research before you write!

From: Maddox
Subject: Re: Think again!
Whales are the #1 killer of sailors and that's a fact.

From: Ashley
Subject: Re: Think again!
Nope, you're thinking of jellyfish. I've seen a picture of a cat kissing a beluga whale and a whale with a diver.

From: Maddox
Subject: Re: Think again!
Might wanna check your facts. Just because you've seen a picture of a whale with a cat or a scuba-diver doesn't mean either survived the encounter. They were probably killed immediately after that picture was taken.

From: Ashley
Subject: Re: Think again!
Yeah right. Get YOUR facts straight!

From: Maddox
Subject: Re: Think again!
Whales are vicious killers. See for yourself!

From: Ashley
Subject: Re: Think again!
The whale is being KILLED BY HUMANS . . . now they seem like vicious creatures! Oh and in case you couldn't tell it's called sarcasm. Watch blackfish you idiot.

From: Maddox
Subject: Re: Think again!
Blackfish is a fictional movie with three writer credits. When whales aren't killing humans, they're drinking all our fresh sea

water, killing turtles, jelly fish, dolphins, and wreaking havoc on our ecosystem.

From: Maddox
Subject: Re: Think again! [2 days later]
I actually looked into it and I think you might be right. I may have overstated the number of people whales kill. I think I owe you an apology.

From: Ashley
Subject: Re: Think again!
You know what I will accept your apology but you have to say whales are majestic, beautiful, and you were wrong.

From: Maddox
Subject: Re: Think again!
Whales are majestic, beautiful and you were wrong.

From: Ashley
Subject: Re: Think again!
FUCK YOU

Whales Are Lazy Animals with Unearned Reputations

When people discuss whales, they often use lofty language to describe their majesty. But does anyone ever stop to ask why? The only noteworthy thing about a whale is its size. Who gives a shit? Notice how the word "majestic" only gets traipsed about when something large is contemplated? People call elephants, oceans and even mountains "majestic." Why? Mountains are collections of boulders, boulders are collections of rocks, and rocks are collections of dirt. I have dirt under my fingernails, and I don't see anyone staring at them breathlessly.

If you shrank a whale down to the size of a mackerel, it'd just be an ugly fish. But as soon as that pale-gray, barnacle-caked monstrosity is larger than a school bus, it's suddenly noted for its grandeur. I'm not impressed by an animal that (A) doesn't have shoes, and (B) couldn't tie them anyway. Whales don't have feet, footwear, or an entire shoe industry. Or any industry. What exactly do whales make, other than blubber? And they're not even good at providing that, because we have to kill them to get it. Imagine if you went to work every day, and your boss had to kill you in order to extract value from you. That's what whales are like: employees you have to kill, except they don't even reproduce fast enough to deliver value sustainably.

At this point, you may think that I have contempt for whales, but I don't. It's hard to have contempt for an animal that matters so little. People say whales are smart and that they can communicate, but who cares? Build a call center, then I'll be impressed. Humans have built pizza shops inside airports. You can buy a ticket to fly to another country, and then while you're waiting for your flight, you can order a piping-hot pizza, made with fresh ingredients grown all over the world, to satiate your peckishness before you experience the miracle of flight in a man-made airplane. Meanwhile, whales are getting tangled up in giant, conspicuous nets. Nets don't even move, they just sit there. Getting caught in a net is like hitting a parked car: embarrassing. One look at a whale's face refutes its regal reputation (Fig. 3).

I'm not suggesting the wholesale slaughter of whales. I don't see the point, because man has better shit to do. I'm suggesting that maybe if whales are so great, we should let them fend for themselves. It's time for whales to either step up or shut up. If

Fig. 3: Whales are gape-mouthed morons!

they can't hack it, that's fine. I don't expect all animals to be able to adapt successfully to the encroachment of mankind. But that failure should come with some loss of reputation. We should stop heralding whales as majestic and start calling them what they really are: idiotic, unproductive, sea losers.

FUCK TABLES

What is a table other than a raised floor? I'd sooner put things on the floor than a table, because at least floors are honest. They're not pretending to be anything they're not. There is no number of legs you can put on a table to make it useful, other than zero. A floor is the people's table. If I wanted a raised floor, I'd just get stairs. Stairs go higher than tables, without ever pretending not to be floors. Imagine going to the house of someone who doesn't have stairs. How do you get to the second level? It won't be with a table. Stairs are so important that they name the whole area of the house "upstairs." Stairs are better at being tables than tables are. The ideal use for a table would be to take an ax to it and then use the planks of wood to bludgeon the person who made the table, for wasting our lives with bullshit.

My entire adult life, I've never owned a table. Every time I point out that I don't have any tables, everyone asks the same question: "How do you eat?" With plates, idiot. Ever heard of them? Plates are just small tables that you can carry. What is a table but an oversized plate that you put other plates on? When you use a plate as a table, you will finally be liberated from the tyranny of raised flooring. When you realize that approximately 50 percent of the foods we eat—such as pizza, sandwiches, fruit and candy—

don't even require so much as a plate, much less a table, that's when you as a human will truly set your spirit free. Buddha spent a lifetime finding enlightenment, yet he failed to include in his sutras a single word about how tables are for dipshits.

Imagine if you had shelves in your house that you used only a few times per week, for a few minutes at a time. People would stone you to death for being such a dumb sonofabitch. Well, that's exactly what you're doing with a table. Unlike most things you put on shelves, meals only last for a few minutes—or up to an hour at most, and that's *if* you have a nosy dinner guest who can't stop asking about your life. Not having a table helps such guests to feel less welcome, and every time a guest feels unwelcome it's another opportunity to be alone. Being alone is awesome.

If you're looking for evidence of the unease we feel for owning tables, look no further than the "centerpiece." A table looks barren without something on it. We all feel it. The glaring omission of something—anything—on a table makes us feel uncomfortable. Deep down, it mirrors the emptiness we feel inside. The more tables you own, the worse your mental state will be. No thanks. I don't want to peer into the chasm of emptiness that is my life every time I look at my useless kitchen furniture. I have a family to help me do that.

Even when people try to find a novel justification for a table, such as a table devoted entirely to a game, it feels absurd. One such contrivance is a "pool table" (Fig. 4).

This was invented by some enterprising idiot who tried to look less stupid in front of his or her friends by giving a table an actual use.

If I wanted to play pool, I'd just put holes in the floor and call it golf. Pool tables are giant and expensive, permanently taking up a huge area of your house, and owners of the tables lose their

Fig. 4: Pool is just raised golf.

minds when you spill spaghetti on them. Ever see anyone lose his or her mind when you spill marinara on the floor? No, of course not. That's because floor owners are chill, and pool-table owners are uptight assholes.

If a squatter proposed to take up 5 percent of your house for the rest of your life, you'd pop him in his stupid horse-mouth. Yet that's exactly what we do by housing a table. If you live in a 500-square-foot studio apartment and the average table size is 24 square feet, and your rent is $1,000, that translates to a cost of $50 per month, or $600 per year, to house your shitty table. It's essentially an area of the apartment you can no longer utilize. If every household in America saved the money wasted every year on buying and housing tables, we'd reduce the national deficit to zero overnight.

For those occasions when you eat something that requires some assembly, like fajitas,* where you need to have multiple

---

* An obnoxious food item that's basically a taco you assemble yourself, with meat, onions, salsa, and all the normal stuff you'd put into a taco. It's marketed as a "fun" food item, but there's nothing fun about assembling your own taco. Not one damn thing.

small dishes to make your fussy meal, a simple food tray will suffice. A food tray is the fajita table of a thinking man. It's a bigger plate that you can put other plates on, except that—unlike the massive plate that is a table—a food tray can be conveniently stored under your bed when you're done eating and you go back to contemplating how awesome your life has become since you've given up tables. It's time to liberate yourself from the tyranny of tables and the dinner guests they attract, and start living the life you deserve—alone.

FUCK HORSES

I hate horses, but I love glue. I wish someone would invent a time machine so all the horses currently in existence or any horse that has ever existed could be rendered into glue. Glue is the most useful and versatile adhesive ever made. Still, fuck horses.

Ever wonder why "beating a dead horse" is a phrase? Because beating it while alive isn't enough. The expression has come to describe any activity that is pointless to continue. Many noted horse haters take issue with this characterization, because beating a dead horse is an end unto itself. Nobody asks an artist why he paints, or why a bonsai gardener arranges potted trees in aesthetically pleasing ways. Similarly, the artistic expression, relaxation and satisfaction one can derive from beating a horse beyond expiration should not be overlooked.

There's a horse-beating simulation game that was released in 2010 called *Red Dead Redemption*. In it, the protagonist is ostensibly tasked with bringing a gang of bandits to justice. However, to all but the least careful observer, it becomes apparent that the real goal in this game is to kill every last horse. It's a brilliant video game, in that it allows the player free rein to dispatch horses in a sandbox of unlimited options. Upon experimentation with the game, one can find many rewarding ways to kill horses: drowning, launching from the back of a wagon, leaving on a train track, jumping off a cliff, running into a tree at full speed, shooting in the back of the head while riding, leaving in a bear den, incineration via Molotov cocktail, or simply shooting in the face with a shotgun. It's even possible to skin a horse for trade or spite. Note that horse skin has virtually no value, just like the animal it once contained.

Here's a detailed list of reasons to hate horses:

Their Stupid Heads

A horse head is mathematically stupid. The average proportions are approximately 26 inches long to 14 inches high, resulting in the queer ratio of 1.9:1, which has no geometric or mathematical significance. An equine face is like the cover of a trashy pulp novel: meaty where you don't want it to be and egregiously hairy. The default expression on a horse's mug is that of a blurry-eyed dope after one too many drinks (Fig. 5).

Fig. 5: Dumbshit horse sticking its goofy tongue out of its meaty lips, like a gummy purse full of teeth.

Teeth

One look at the long, toothy grin of a horse tells you all you need to know about the animal: Nobody is home. Often, a shit-eating grin is the reason people are beaten in the street. A horse will keep grinning no matter what you do to it, even when beaten beyond death, hence the famous expression (Fig. 6).

Fig. 6: Even in death, horses grin like morons.

Diet

Horses subsist on a diet consisting entirely of charity carrots, sugar cubes and weeds. In spite of this purely donated, exclusively vegetarian diet, horse shit smells infinitely worse than human shit. If ever there was an argument to shut down a vegetarian's claim that shit from a vegetable-based diet doesn't stink, horses are proof positive that they're full of shit—and that shit smells.

Many cities in America have open-carriage horse rides around parks or town squares. These are marketed as romantic activities for couples who want to do something quaint and clichéd, like cuddle in warm blankets while some poor coach-man parades them around in exchange for a meager living. This is all while the couple is huffing a constant jet-stream of horse manure that's being collected in a satchel behind the horse. It's like a mobile sewage plant that blocks traffic for people who made far superior transportation choices, like cars, bikes, or not leaving the house.

Feet

When you eliminate speed, convenience and smell as reasons people might choose an open-carriage ride, that leaves the novelty of the sound horseshoes make while clopping about on city streets. I don't get it, but some people find annoying sounds pleasing, like whale songs or children's laughter. So here's a simple solution: Get a CD of a horse clopping. Or play the sound of horses walking on your mobile device. You can have all the convenience of twenty-first-century automotive technology while still listening to the sounds of fifteenth-century transportation. There's no reason to keep the actual horses around.

Eyes

Ever heard of a fly cap? Of course not, because you're not a horse. If you were, you'd be illiterate and incapable of reading the question. A fly cap is a meshed net used to cover a horse's eyes to protect them from flies. Because horses are apparently too stupid to blink, some enterprising human came along and invented a device to prevent flies from landing in a horse's eyes. I thought that invention already existed, called "eyelids."

Another type of eye cover for horses is the blinder. These have two uses: (1) So the horse knows to go only straight forward, instead of wandering off a cliff somewhere; and (2) so they don't get scared, thinking the carriage is chasing them. Horses don't understand how wagons work, so they need industrious humans to invent devices to trick them, and it doesn't take much.

Skin

The skin on a horse's face looks like an uncircumcised penis. Its lower lip droops like a loose slice of roast beef (Fig. 5), and the skin on its body feels like a cross between a peach and a fish: fuzzy, and it can be petted in only one direction. What a garbage animal.

Body

A horse's eyes are too big for its face. Its face is too big for its head. Its skeleton is too small for its body. None of the proportions on a horse make sense, and this is never more apparent than when one observes a horse's skeleton (Fig. 7). The equine skeleton looks like it belongs to an animal with a much smaller frame, like a Chihuahua. Its spine tapers off with a whimper. Its hobbled hind legs dispirit even those with the most resolute constitution. Every jockey should be required to observe a horse's skeleton before riding one, in order to make an informed decision about whether or not they want to sit on such a dumb, malformed pot of future-glue. The only redeeming quality of the horse's body is its ribs, which look like they'd probably taste great with a smoky sauce.

An equid is a hoofed animal with slender legs and a flat coat, and an equidiot is anyone who likes equids. Horses are constantly

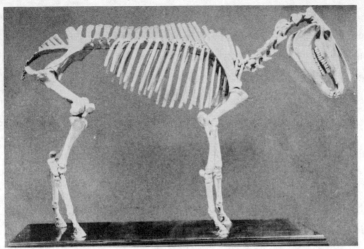

Fig. 7: A horse's skeleton looks like a small, spooky dog.

trying to masquerade themselves as something else, as anyone would in similar circumstances. Make no mistake, the following animals are all horses:

Ponies

Ponies are just smaller horses. A casual horse hater might think that ponies are less worthy of our vitriol, since there's less horse to hate. But a rational person hates ponies more because they're harder to hit with a cannon. Speaking of cannons, a horse is the dumbest animal to ride into battle because they get scared easily and hop up on their hind legs like giant, penis-faced meerkats with knobby legs.

Giraffes

A giraffe is just a taller horse. There are countless nature documentaries that lionize giraffes by describing how fierce they can be with their kicks. Big deal, kicks aren't impressive. Know what is? Broadswords. I can take out any giraffe with a broadsword. I don't even need to look. I can be blindfolded and just wave the broadsword above my head, swinging wildly. With a broadsword and enough time, I can turn any nature preserve into a cemetery.

Zebras

Zebras are the tigers of the equine world, except, unlike tigers, I can't stop thinking about running them over in my jeep. Tigers have stripes, because they need to sneak up on prey. The stripes help them blend in to their environment. Zebras have stripes because they're the child molesters of the animal kingdom, and they need to blend in prison.

Camels

A camel is just a desert horse. This may be the most controversial horse on the list because of the hump on the camel's back. But giraffes have humps on their backs too. They're pretty much the exact same animal (Fig. 8).

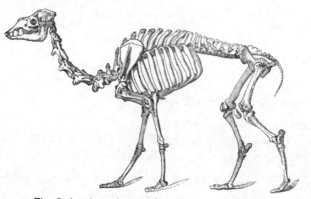

Fig. 8: Look at this goofy, scoop-necked idiot.

DID YOU KNOW?
My contract with the publisher specifies
the use of horse glue to bind this book.

In some countries like the United States, eating horses is frowned upon, because some jerks like to pet them. However, men of hardier spirit in countries like Canada, Mexico, Spain and France eat horsemeat with extreme prejudice. That is to say, horses are more likely to be eaten than not, when they're spotted in the wild or captivity. Some horse owners prefer to put their horses in stables, but the best place for a horse is between two slices of brioche, chewed up in small satisfying bites that slowly turn to poop in my butt. Passing digested horse stool is the ultimate justice for such a malodorous animal. I posit here that digested horse stool is less disagreeable to the olfactory senses than horse manure itself.

Since there haven't been any long, protracted world wars in over half a century, horses are no longer being used as bullet sponges on the battlefield. Even if you object to eating a horse—because you're a pussy—eating them makes sense from an environmental standpoint:

**Environmental Advantages to
Eating Every Single Horse**

1. People are starving, and horses are edible. If there are horses that aren't starving, and humans who are, it doesn't take a genius to connect the dots. But it sure doesn't hurt that I am one.

2. Horses are warm-blooded, and their bodies radiate heat energy into space. So in a literal sense, horses are space heaters contributing to global warming. The best place to put a horse heater, so it won't emit any more heat, is the bottom of the sea with the whales or, failing that, a catapult.

3. Horses take up space, and the space they occupy necessarily occupies some measurable amount of air, land, or water. That's air, land or water that could be used by other, nonhorse beings or objects with greater value, like rats or medical waste.

Speaking of medical waste, I'd rather ride a pile of used syringes than a horse.

FUCK TREES

It boggles my mind that nobody has coined a phrase that describes the opposite of a "tree hugger." I'm going to do it here and now: "tree puncher." Every tree I see is a tree I want to cold-cock. In life, there are two things: paths and obstacles. Trees aren't paths, so they must be obstacles—unless you actually want to climb a tree, in which case they are paths . . . to nothing. But I didn't evolve opposable thumbs and a taste for whiskey so I could climb a wooden pole in a forest. Climbing a tree is one of the worst things you can do with your time, ranking just above cutting yourself and below listening to a whale sing. Fuck whales.

Nothing good comes from trees, except food. But there aren't enough food-baring trees for them to matter. There exist over 100,000 tree species in the world, and of them, only about fifty produce any food—and that's including things that are barely food, like nuts and olives. That's 0.0005 percent of trees. If the same ratio of humans were productive, we'd all have died centuries ago, and you wouldn't be reading this book. Trees are freeloaders, and their roots literally leach nutrients from the planet. When you kill a tree, you're returning stolen elements back to the Earth. Trees are nature's hoarders.

I use a lot of wood, because I hate trees. One of the main reasons I wrote this book is to kill more trees for paper and horses for glue. As far as wood goes, there are far better materials with which to build, such as concrete and steel. Give me a concrete bed with a steel frame any day over a wooden one. The only reason I sleep on a bed with a wooden frame is my contempt for trees. Every person who has ever argued with me about the merits of trees owns wooden furniture, so their so-called love of trees rings hollow. If you love trees so much, sit on the floor.* I sit on wooden chairs for the same reason I ride horses: I like putting my ass on things I hate.

The best product you can give to a fellow tree-hater is a box of toothpicks, because it's a tree product wrapped in another tree product. That's like a steak wrapped in a bigger steak. Or better yet, keep the toothpicks for yourself: When your friend asks for one, throw them away right in front of him. That way you kill a tree while simultaneously losing a friend. Friends are horrible.

In Shel Silverstein's *The Giving Tree*, Silverstein tells a story about a tree that gives everything it has to some ungrateful kid who keeps using the tree and asking it for more, and the tree keeps falling for it like a sucker. Even in a fictional universe where a tree can be anthropomorphic and have any personality the author wants to give it, trees tend to have the personalities of saps. Any adjective used to describe a tree when applied to a human is neutral at best and negative at worst. For example, calling someone's acting "wooden" implies stiffness and rigidity. Trees can't act for shit.

People talk about the "root of a problem," or the "roots of your hair," which, if visible, means you've done a shitty job of dyeing it. Steak that sucks is described as being "tough as bark." When you're

---

* The thinking man's table.

confused or perplexed, you've been "stumped." "Scrub" means low shrubs, as well as an unaccomplished loser, hanging out the passenger side of his best friend's ride.

As with horses and tables, trees occupy space. They defy our most basic liberty: the right to exist. Existence starts with taking up some amount of space, and trees are among the most egregious space hogs on Earth, right after whales. Every tree that exists necessarily means a human can't occupy that same space. When trees aren't displacing humans, they're preventing valuable energy from reaching Earth, in the form of sunlight. Beneath every tree is a shadow.

Tree apologists will argue that the trade-off for the energy they absorb is that trees produce oxygen for us to breathe. No thanks. Humans breathe approximately 1,631 pounds of oxygen per year,[2] and it takes roughly seven or eight trees to produce enough oxygen for just one human. Trees suck at the one thing we supposedly need them to do, and anyone who thinks humans need trees to produce oxygen is an idiot. Case in point: space stations. Astronauts can live in space stations for years without the aid of trees, by electrolyzing water. The solar energy stolen by leaves in exchange for a paltry amount of oxygen could be better used to produce electricity to separate oxygen molecules from water. This process even gives us hydrogen as a byproduct, which we can use for fuel. Every last tree should be replaced with a solar panel. The energy we gain could be used to power robots to harvest raw materials to make more useful things, like metal bedframes and concrete pyramids. Covering Earth in pyramids would effectively turn our planet into a giant spiked morning star. That would be badass. If we ever played planetary chicken with an alien world, they'd think twice before they rammed their lumpy extraterrestrial turd into our totally sick, spiked planet.

There have been roughly half a dozen people orbiting Earth for the better part of this decade. If we needed trees to produce enough oxygen for them, we wouldn't have room for any scientific instruments aboard our space stations. We'd just have a jumbled mess of equipment with shitty trees poking out from every direction, hurtling through space. Kind of like a smaller version of Earth. Humans can take trees into space, but trees can't take us anywhere, except up, and at the excruciatingly slow growth rate of half a foot per year. It's not that trees don't aspire to reach space; they do. But much like producing oxygen, they're terrible at it. The world's tallest trees only reach a height of three hundred feet, and it takes them about six hundred years to get there. The start of outer space is 327,360 feet from the surface of Earth. So if you relied on trees to get you into space, it'd take six hundred years and you'd still have another 327,060 feet to go. Garbage.

Not only do trees stand in defiance of our right to exist, but they also stand in defiance of another one of our most basic liberties: the right to move. No matter your mode of transportation, be it on land, air, or water, trees present themselves as giant, shitty obstacles, there only for you to crash into. Birds fly into them and die all the time. Trees are birds' natural enemies. Ever wonder why birds prefer to sit on man-made objects like power lines, in spite of the mortal risk posed by half a million volts? It's because trees are teeming with ants, spiders, sap and other creepy bullshit that can bite, sting or trap you in amber for scientists to discover millions of years from now. Risking electrocution is a better fate than being encased in an amber sarcophagus or having ants crawl all over you.

The only places on Earth where humans aren't impeded by the arboreal scourge are the polar caps and the high seas: environments the hardiest of men gravitate toward and thrive in. If it weren't for whales in the sea, it'd be a perfect habitat for rugged humans. We could live happily on concrete and steel drilling platforms, free from the tyranny of trees. As it stands now, the polar caps are a perfect home base from which to wage war on trees and whales. The arctic remains our closest approximation to a utopian ideal, in which humans can live in peace and comfort.

FUCK FAMILIES

Families are collections of strangers. You have nothing in common with your parents and siblings other than a fraction of your genetic code. Who gives a shit? Being that we share 99.9 percent of our DNA with every other person on Earth, saying that you're related to any one person is statistically equivalent to saying you're related to every other human being. Hell, we share 96 percent of our genetic code with a chimpanzee and 60 percent with a banana,[3] but I don't see anyone expecting me to buy expensive plane tickets to visit a passive-aggressive plantain over the holidays. When we are born, we don't know our fathers or mothers any more than we know the doctor who delivers us—maybe a little less, since we meet the doctor first.

At some point in his life, your dad was just some guy you didn't know. He was a sexless loser masturbating to bra ads in a magazine. He probably had pimples and bad breath, and was rightfully insecure about getting laid. At some point in his life, he probably had dating trouble and premature ejaculation. He was rejected by a dozen or more women before he met your mother and settled, or she settled on him, or—almost by definition—they both settled for each other. Your dad lived a life full of mistakes, regrets and accidents before he had you, and in all likelihood he hasn't told you about them. Your dad has presented a curated version of himself to you. This version probably omits poor gambling decisions, bad investments and betrayal of someone's trust at some point or another. Your dad may have been a shoplifter, vandal, arsonist or murderer. There's no guarantee that your dad was a good or decent person. When the only narrator telling you the full story of his life is him, this version of events is unreliable at best.

The point is, your father is an arbitrary person. He chose to have you (maybe); you definitely didn't choose to have him. He's just a guy who decided to bang your mom, because he was horny and she was there. Before you were born, if given the choice—as well as the ability to divorce yourself from any childhood memories that might bias you—you might not pick that person to be your father at all.

The notion that we owe loyalty to our families is not only absurd and unfounded but also damaging to our personal growth. In the name of family, people tend to suffer through incredible levels of toxic behavior. Because of some antiquated notion of familial or tribal bond, family members are often expected to stick together despite all kinds of physical, emotional and verbal abuse. No thanks.

Your family members know all your weaknesses. They know which buttons to push to set you off, and sometimes they'll use these triggers to manipulate you. Famously, mothers are master manipulators. They will withhold their affection if you don't check in frequently enough or present them with the right kind of gifts. Their loyalty is for sale, and they will strike you from their good graces the second they feel like you aren't measuring up to their expectations. Mothers are able to wield their ailments—real or perceived—to garner sympathy points from their kids. These facts are so well known they are the bedrock dynamics of TV sitcoms.

When you realize that your family is full of assholes and strangers, it frees you to treat its members like you would any other asshole or stranger: with dismissal. You wouldn't put up with a stranger's bullshit, so why would you put up with it from a family member?

Families can't be trusted to have your best interests in mind, considering how selfishly they behave. In many European, Asian and Middle Eastern countries, extended families live together by design, so that the family elders always have their kids around to take care of them. Rather than hire hospice workers, these old people decide to create them. Their retirement plan amounts to raising a staff of indentured servants. That's not only selfish and inefficient, it's downright creepy.

No percentage of someone's destiny should include providing unpaid hospice care. By making that decision for you before you were born, your parents greatly limit your potential to become something that might require a skill set beyond wiping asses, like being a Mars colonist. Your parents are holding back humanity.

Never Trust a Compliment Coming from Your Mother

If parents are supposed to love you unconditionally, when your mom gives you a compliment, you necessarily can't trust it. There's at least a 50 percent chance she's lying to you. You can program a robot to tell you that it loves you every day, but it doesn't mean anything because you know there's no other possible outcome. A mom's compliment is as meaningless as it is boring. Give me a mom who challenges you to a duel, and I'll show you a mom who's worth discovering. I would love to box a mom. Hand-to-hand combat is a great way to show how much you love your child because you're giving him the best gift in life: the ability to survive.

Siblings are a toss-up. Occasionally, a sibling can become a friend, with the exact same likelihood as making a friend out of a random stranger. But, as with a stranger, equally possible is a sibling who becomes your mortal enemy. This person will know all your weaknesses, insecurities and where you live. But unlike a regular mortal enemy, he or she will hold your relatedness over your head. You have to see this person at least once or twice a year at family gatherings, and he or she is fifth in line to be your surrogate decision maker if you're ever admitted to a hospital unconscious. But that's not the worst-case scenario. What tops it is having a mortal enemy who's also your conjoined twin. Having a regular, nonenemy conjoined twin wouldn't be so bad if society still had the need for dual-scimitar-wielding guardians stationed outside caves full of jewels. But having a conjoined twin who's also your mortal enemy would be the closest approximation to a living hell. On the balance, siblings just aren't worth the risk.

We are all programmed from a young age to feel obligated to help out family in need. But since you are 99.9 percent related to the homeless veteran down the street, isn't he far more deserving than your shitty dad with a gambling problem? Why bail your alcoholic brother out of jail for getting arrested in a strip club when you could use those same funds to help a plucky orphan with a gifted vocal range? When you consider that by merely having a genetic relationship with someone, you are 30 percent more likely to be sexually abused by that person,[4] aren't these the last people who deserve your help?

Fuck families.

FUCK CUPCAKES

Cupcakes are the pretzels of desserts: You always tire of eating them before you run out. Dessert platters everywhere bow beneath the weight of cupcakes nobody wants. Cupcakes are the manifesto of the contemptuous baker. When determining whether or not something is shitty, a quick rule of thumb is to gauge how many apologists it has. For example, finding a vaunted "good" Philly cheesesteak requires both a divining rod and a residence in Philadelphia, because apparently only locals know where the "real" good Philly cheesesteaks are. You can't just ask someone or look it up online, because if you didn't like what you ate, the apologist will claim you asked the wrong person or went to the wrong place. Rarely do geniuses like myself come along and question whether or not the food item in question could even be good to begin with. When we look at the cheesesteak critically, it's easy to spot the problem: There are only three ingredients, and one of them is Cheez Whiz. A processed, cheese-flavored canola oil product is one of the three ingredients on this supposedly delicious sandwich. Pass.

Cupcake apologists will argue for days that a "good" cupcake is "worth it." Worth what? Suffering all the bad ones? Cupcakes are essentially just smaller cakes, baked in a muffin tin. There's more surface area in common between the batter and the tin, which causes the batter to dry out. A typical cupcake will suck up every last molecule of moisture within a one-mile radius, which makes them the perfect weapon for fighting whales. But as weapons go, I'd sooner eat an unpinned hand grenade than a cupcake.

The only dessert that gets a free pass for being served in a cup is pudding, or possibly Jell-O, because those desserts are in a semi-fluid state. This is what cups were invented for—fluids.

In iconography, a literal manifestation of the icon would almost always disappoint. If you see a sign for a picnic area, and then you show up to find no seats and only a giant T-shaped slab of a table, few would disapprove of starting a forest fire (Fig. 9). Similarly, a cupcake only represents a fun time. To literally eat one is as disappointing as those giant rainbow lollipops that look like a mouth carnival and taste like nothing.

Fig. 9: A Finnish road sign that, if taken literally, indicates a shitty picnic site with one tree, a giant T-shaped table as thick as a tree trunk, and no seats.

Anything meritorious in a cupcake was stolen from a better dessert. The aesthetically satisfying swirl of frosting is stolen from soft-serve ice cream. The shape is stolen from muffins, the sprinkles are stolen from donuts and even the paper cup is stolen from peanut butter cups. The cupcake is a Frankenstein monster, stitched together by culinary corpse thieves.

Consider the logistics of eating a tiny piece of cake with a pile of frosting on top. It's impossible to consume a cupcake gracefully, because unless you can unhinge your jaw like a python, your nose will slam into a heap of frosting when you bite into it. You look like you just finished blowing a gingerbread man, with his buttercream still dangling from the tip of your nose. Humiliating.

This is such a problem that people have created online guides and strategies for eating cupcakes. Cupcake apologists have suggested everything from using utensils—which defeats the purpose of a portable dessert—to reconstructing the cake portion by cutting it in half and then stacking the bottom third of the dessert on top, creating a sandwich with the frosting in the middle (Fig. 10). So there you have it: The best way to eat a cupcake is to turn it into something entirely different. It's a sandwich cookie, except instead of two rigid wafers competently securing the frosting inside, it's a spongy, crumbly mess that gives me rage sweat.

Fig. 10: Instructions on how to turn a cupcake into an entirely different dessert, which still sucks.

In spite of these glaring shortcomings, pastry chefs refuse to abandon the dessert. Instead, they keep trying to improve it, so it isn't as frustrating to eat. Case in point: the mini-cupcake. A mini-cupcake is a smaller version of a regular cupcake, with its own drawbacks. Instead of being too dry, it has a soupy middle that tastes like elf cum (I'm guessing). The frosting-to-cake ratio is 2:3, which is what you get on a normal cake from the top edge. In other words, it's too much.

When regular cakes were the norm, people would look forward to these occasional bites of frosting overload. It was a refreshing change of pace from the rest of the cake and something of a novelty. Then mini-cupcakes came along and made the novelty mundane. Every bite is an edge bite, and nobody is happier for it.

Even in the rare instance in which a cupcake is baked perfectly—by some miraculous intersection of science, faith and unaccountable luck—the very best cupcake result still isn't as good as the most average of cakes. There is one insurmountable shortcoming: layers. Cakes can be baked in sheets, and each layer can be an entirely different type of cake, with varying flavors, textures and styles. Then those layers can sandwich inventive frostings and fillings that include fresh fruit, creams and jellies, giving bakers the latitude they need to make a dessert that is delicious enough to rival the highest status to which a dessert can aspire: the pie.

There's no point in biting beyond the surface of a cupcake, because you won't encounter anything new at the bottom: only more dry, shitty cake you have to scrape off paper and then off your tongue. The best way to eat a cupcake is to dropkick it into a landfill.

FUCK FOLKSY WISDOM

Folksy wisdom is bullshit. These are the kitschy faux tin signs or "vintage" 1950s posters found in roadside gift shops with sayings on them, like "Curiosity killed the cat." Yeah, well, curiosity also put a man on the moon. Curiosity is the spark that ignites scientific inquiry. If we weren't curious, we would still be in caves, shitting in neat piles while we pick each other's fleas. Minus the caves, because we'd be too scared to go inside and investigate. At which point, we would have died in a field, from exposure to the elements.

These phrases are often blanket philosophies that don't fit in every, or even most, situations. Take, for example, the phrase "You're allowed to fail, you're only human." First of all, why the qualifier "only"? As if there's something higher to aspire to be than a human being. Humans built rocket ships and yo-yos and are the best species known. To say that you're *only* human is to say that you're *only* the best.

Also, why is someone I don't know telling me that I'm "allowed to fail"? Failure isn't something we need special permission to do. It's something most people do all the time. Those people are called failures. They usually fail by not following instructions given by people in charge, who would be the very same people giving them permission to fail. And by the way, what kind of employer would ever tell his or her subordinates that it's okay to fail? Don't want to win? Stay home, idiot.

People use the word "folks" as a populist appeal to the common man: that good old, homegrown, corn-fed, salt-of-the-earth everyperson, who exists only in the idyllic countrysides of our imaginations. Those people we call "folks" are the same boring, backwater boors you find everywhere, including big cities. The only difference is, we fondly lionize the heartland, so the people there don't kill themselves out of a sense of sheer irrelevance.

Some of these quotes make me want to barf on a shark, which is something I've actually done before.* Take, for example, "Don't be afraid to be different." It sounds like something a twinkly-eyed grandpa would say after you came home from a rough day at school. It's easy to mistake it for actual wisdom instead of what it actually is: lazy. It's easy for someone to tell you to "be different" when they're not putting their reputations, careers or relationships on the line. In order to take their advice to heart, all you have to do is overcome the fear and anxiety of being ostracized!

It's one thing to tell someone what to do, it's another to tell them how to do it. Not being afraid to be "different" is the result of personal development, self-reflection and awareness of what it is that makes you different. It also benefits from careful consideration of the possible outcomes of your actions. It's only after all these factors are taken into account that one can have the confidence and peace of mind to venture outside the norm. After all,

---

* Twice. I was in a shark cage in Hawaii and the waters were choppy, so my diet of Spam and coffee right before a rough boat ride, combined with other idiots barfing on the boat, made me lose my otherwise iron constitution. As the captain was feeding the sharks, I threw up three times, and twice I hit the shark as it was feeding. Fuck sharks.

there's another word for being different without fear: reckless. If you're at a bar where everyone is drinking socially, and you decide to overdo it and become a drunk idiot who gropes boobs and starts fights, you'll definitely be "different." You might also wake up in a Dumpster. Being different without regard to the possible outcome is how you start an unexpected career change, to unpaid bus-bench-warmer.

One of the more popular sources of folksy wisdom is Robert Fulghum's book *All I Really Need to Know I Learned in Kindergarten*. The title alone makes me want to go back in time and microwave my dad's balls before he has a chance to impregnate my mom. And/or kill Hitler. Unless they started teaching kindergartners how to drive, do algebra and check condoms for holes, there's plenty for you to learn *after* kindergarten. Five-year-olds don't know shit about the dangers of bigotry and fascism, the rights of citizens, or the limits of government. Kids don't know not to touch their genitals after chopping jalapeños, the importance of vaccination, or when to clap at the symphony. In fact, most knowledge that we need to stay alive, healthy and satisfied as adults is learned years after kindergarten.

One such bit of knowledge from Fulghum's book is to "share everything." It's stupid advice, because there are tons of things we shouldn't share: bad stock tips, gossip, needles, STDs, snot rags and babies. Nobody wants to hold your baby. Holding a baby is like holding a Fabergé egg: All you can think about is how pissed off everyone would be if you accidentally dropped it.

Then there's this gem: "Don't hit people." Sometimes people need to be punched right in their stupid ape mouths. If someone is standing up in the middle of a plane with a bomb vest, you'd best put your foot up his ass and break it off in his colon for good measure. Show me a kindergarten that teaches kids how to chokeslam a terrorist, and I'll show you a kindergarten that's about to get a beefy new student who hates horses.

Perhaps at the top of the turd stack is this nauseatingly wholesome suggestion: "Warm cookies and cold milk are good for you." If your goal is to become a lardass, then go for it, by all means. Fulghum opines about how much better the world would be if we all ate milk and cookies and then lay down "with our blankies for a nap." I'm not sleeping on the floor like a stable animal. Even baby Jesus managed to get a bed of straw in the year 0 B.C. in a manger in the Middle East. And who the hell calls it a "blankie"? Grow up, you stupid cow. And before you get your panties all wadded up into an anxiety-drenched mess, I'm not so obtuse as to miss the implication that "warm cookies and cold milk" are good for your "soul" or spirit or whatever idiotic metaphysical force you believe in. I know what was meant by the quote, but it's good for neither. Also, objectively, cold cookies are the best, because they're perfect for dunking into coffee or tea. That's just another thing you don't know if you're a clueless dipshit kid with an overinflated sense of importance due to aggrandizing lists like these. Adults rule.

The only reason there even exists such a list is that an adult wrote it, in a language that adults created, on paper milled by adults. How's this for a folksy saying: "Kids don't build anything and should shut the fuck up."

Often, these corny homespun tidbits are not only stupid and bereft of wisdom, but they're contradictory. Take, for example, the quote "It's never too late to learn." Sounds inspiring, especially to geriatrics who are prone to feeling the pangs of regret later in life. That is, until you read that "You can't teach an old dog new tricks." Oops! And let's not forget that "Clothes make the man"— unless you happen to subscribe to the notion that "It's what's on the inside that counts." So what counts is what's on the inside and outside. Got it. And what about this universal truism about caution: "You should look before you leap." Unless you consider the phrase "A moment of hesitation causes a lifetime of regret."

If you're feeling like a bag of assholes after reading this chapter, don't feel too down on yourself. After all, nobody is perfect. Unless you practice, because practice makes perfect. Fuck folksy wisdom.

FUCK SILHOUETTE PHOTOS

Nobody needs to see another dark palm tree outline against a sunset. Shadows were a novel concept at the age of three. By now we get it. Any phenomenon that occurs naturally every twenty-four hours, 365 days per year—plus every time you occlude light with an object—isn't noteworthy.

There are billions of these pictures already cluttering the pages of cruise ship brochures. These brochures attract people who go on vacation, see palm trees during a sunset and take even more silhouette photos. Then they sit back, thinking "Nailed it! Looks just like the brochure." They post it on social networks for all their friends to envy, which causes all of them to go on cruises of their own and take even more silhouette photos.

Like a virus, each silhouette picture spawns a thousand more. The ease of taking photos of dark subjects in front of bright backdrops, and the tasteful simplicity of the contrast that results, gives the photographer a powerful hit of dopamine, which makes taking these photos nearly irresistible. As a creator, I can attest to the psychological high one gets when realizing an artistic vision. But if pros and amateurs alike can take perfect silhouette photos, the variable that distinguishes the pro from the amateur—talent—becomes irrelevant.

The one saving grace for the silhouette photo is nude photography. If you're taking a silhouette photo, and you're not showing nipples, what's your problem? Professionals and amateurs alike blow opportunities like this daily. I've spent countless minutes zooming in on vacation bikini silhouette photos to determine whether the bikini is, in fact, present. This metric predicts for everything from marriage proposals to scandals. When casually glancing through the endless photo-dump of friends' vacation photos, seeing one of these posted by a friend who was previously single could signal a burgeoning new relationship. It can be useful to know this information, to budget for yet another pain-in-the-ass destination wedding your friend will be having two or three years from the exact moment that photo was taken. But still, fuck silhouette photos.

FUCK FICTIONAL SERIALS

Game of Thrones is one of the most popular fantasy dramas of the last two decades, and it's the ultimate platform for nerds to be outraged at those not participating. Everywhere you go, from parties and watercooler discussions to forums, operating rooms, and Seders, there are mobs of fantasy zealots judging you for not being invested in their make-believe universe.

The television show is based on the seven-book series A Song of Ice and Fire, by famed fantasy author George R. R. Martin. All the books combined—both published and announced—contain around 5,600 pages, which at a conservative figure of 350 words per page, and an average adult reading-rate of 200 words per minute, it'd take roughly 163 hours to read the entire series. Even watching the series takes a significant investment in time, as there are 8 seasons, released or announced, with around 10 hour-long episodes per season, so that's an investment of 80 hours to be "caught up" on what's happening.

I'd sooner inject concrete into my boner than watch *Game of Thrones* beginning to end. Nothing against the series; what I've seen of it is good. The acting is competent and the writing is great. In fact, all of the hallmark features of a quality series are there: good direction, lighting, cinematography, effects and plot twists to keep audiences intrigued. So why refuse to watch it? Because I'm not spending 80 hours of my life learning the detailed history, politics, geography and culture of people who never existed. In interviews, Martin said his series was inspired by the fifteenth-century Wars of the Roses, an actual thing that happened.[5]

You could enroll in a class on Tudor history at Boston University and complete an entire semester's worth of lectures in 33 hours.[6] Even if you double the amount of class time for homework and reading to 66 hours, that's still less time than it takes to watch *Game of Thrones*. You can learn the history of actual people and real wars, including the real wars that influenced the fictional people of Westeros having fictional wars, in less time than it takes for you to watch the fantasy version.

When friends decide to watch *Game of Thrones* in social settings, I watch any episode and season they happen to be watching. I don't think people deserve to be deprived of my presence just because they're losers who watch fantasy soap operas instead of doing something interesting. It doesn't bother me that I'm watching out of sequence, because (A) I don't care, and (B) I'm an adult with the ability to infer what's going on based on contextual clues. I know that when two people tense up around each other, they have some bad blood between them. I don't need to know what that is, because living on this Earth and being around other humans, I've been able to pick up on social cues and can apply those cues to similar settings. While it doesn't bother me that I'm watching midstride, it really seems to bother ardent fans—a lot. People who care about fictional serials can't seem to wrap their heads around how anyone could enjoy something without knowing every single detail of every character.

It's even worse when the same standard is applied to serialized comedies, where the characters make lots of inside jokes and references to old episodes. If a comedy requires you to do homework and research about the series to understand the jokes, it's probably not very good. A callback to a previous episode should be one tool in a comedy writer's arsenal, not the primary device for delivering humor.

If the same standard were applied for people, you'd have to learn every single detail of every person you meet to understand their motivations for doing anything. Sounds preposterous? That's because it is. You don't need to know a person's entire history to make a value judgment on his character. In fact, most people can tell a lot about one another at a glance.

People have likened my midstride philosophy to someone listening to a record by dropping the needle down in the middle of a track. I couldn't agree more, because that's exactly what it's like: still enjoyable. If listening to half of a song wasn't enjoyable, radio stations couldn't exist. Radio stations rely on people scanning through the dial to find a song they like. The song is rarely at the start of the track, but in spite of this, people still tune in and listen because they like the song or the genre of music. Watching a series from the middle is exactly the same. Suggesting that we shouldn't consume a series partially is akin to suggesting that we shouldn't try a bite of someone's meal because we wouldn't enjoy it as much as eating their entire dinner. That's idiotic, and so are these nerdy fantasy losers.

FUCK POETRY

Nothing is worse than poetry.* Poetry was created by ancient, unsophisticated people with primitive entertainment. For fun, they had to while away their time creating "word art" and twirling their skirts at harvest festivals. They didn't have television, video games, computers or submarines with which to amuse themselves. Poetry was invented by people so bereft of entertainment that they made a big deal over things like the sun, moon and rain. Rain makes me want to piss and then puts me to sleep. There's nothing duller than rain, except poetry.

Almost every culture in the world has a rich poetic tradition that is equal parts pretentious and boring. Poetry fans and lecturers use jargon like "phonoaesthetics," or the allegedly pleasing quality of words and phrases, as a justification for why poetry has any value. Know what is actually pleasing to listen to? Music. Poetry is songs without the music. Everyone knows that the worst part of any song is the lyrics. Most of the music I listen to is devoid of lyrics. The last thing I want when I'm listening to a good toe-tapper is some jackass spinning a yarn in my ear. Save it for your college application, nerd-lord, I'm

---

* Except whales.

trying to relax with some music, not have you jack off my ear with words.

What's so important that you need to interrupt my music to tell me about it? I can't think of anything so pressing that you should write it down, make it rhyme and then interrupt me with it during a song. Just text it to me. Or better yet, text it to yourself and throw your phone in the ocean. Lyrics are garbage. The people who write them are just thinly disguised poets, trying to cram their flowery language into every facet of our lives every chance they get. Fortune cookies were invented by poets, so they could sneak more of their goofy words into our food. The entire children's bedtime story industry has been taken over by these bloviating bards, and they've even infiltrated the bottle caps of sports drinks. You can't escape these obnoxious, word-gilding lilies.

Poets pride themselves on their use of symbolism. Using symbols is inherently sneaky, creepy and dishonest, or, at the very least, not forthright. Symbolism is like being at a party with people who are having a conversation in front of you with too many inside references that only they understand or care about. The point of language is to communicate ideas clearly, not sneak hidden meaning into your messages. You're not a prisoner of war. Stop trying to smuggle hidden dispatches and just say what you mean and mean what you say.

Poetry doesn't give, it takes. You have to do a little mental gymnastics every time you hear a poetic phrase or verse, which is exhausting. Like the worst art, the worst poetry requires us to do the most interpretation. Did the author mean to relate grains of sand to time, or was she recalling a literal memory about sand? Is the cold a metaphor for unrequited love, death, the loss of enthusiasm, or is it just a bit chilly? We live in a world where terrorists could blow up a truck at any moment; nobody has time for this crap.

In 1923, Pulitzer Prize–winning poet Robert Frost published a poem called "Stopping by Woods on a Snowy Evening."[7] It's often cited as one of the top poems of all time for specious reasons:

> *Whose woods these are I think I know.*
> *His house is in the village, though;*
> *He will not see me stopping here*
> *To watch his woods fill up with snow.*

Already off to a rocky start, Frost opines about the owner of the woods. The second line ends in "though" for no reason other than to rhyme with the word "know" from the first line. The phonoaesthetic quality is dubious, as there's a case to be made that adding superfluous words like "though" to the end of sentences may actually erode the pleasing—and subjective—aural quality of the phrase. The third and fourth lines are pure fluff. We gain no further understanding of the alleged owner of the woods. And in order for him to watch the woods fill up with snow, he'd have to stay considerably longer than "stopping by." He goes on:

> *My little horse must think it queer*
> *To stop without a farmhouse near*
> *Between the woods and frozen lake*
> *The darkest evening of the year.*

Here he's speculating about his horse's full adjudication of the facts at hand, which is preposterous given how stupid horses are. He even suggests that his horse is aware of a calendar year and the relative length of days. Also, I have serious reservations about the odds that he coincidentally stopped precisely on the winter solstice.

He gives his harness bells a shake
To ask if there is some mistake. . . .

The horse isn't shaking his bells as if "to ask if there is some mistake." Horses just twitch sometimes. They're garbage animals.

The woods are lovely, dark and deep,
But I have promises to keep,
And miles to go before I sleep,
And miles to go before I sleep.[8]

Literary critics can't even agree on what Frost means with the final repeating lines of the poem. Some speculate that what Frost meant by "sleep" can be interpreted as "the night's rest at the end of the speaker's journey—well earned or troubled, depending on the interpretation—or to the more final rest at the end of the speaker's life."[9] Others have weighed in that it might be a statement about his fatigue in the sense that he's about to "drop off,"[10] or that it's the speaker's denial of the fact that he's already begun to nod off.[11]

Any time writing isn't clear or is open to a lot of interpretation, it's a sign that it wasn't written well. Or is all of this interpretation supposed to be fun? Is it enjoyable to read, reread and decode the same seven words over and over again? The worst movies, like the worst writing, are ones in which the director opts to cut to black in the final scene, without resolving the film's main story arc. It leaves the story's meaning open to interpretation by the viewer. This gives first-year film majors a lot of rhetorical fat to chew in classroom debates that don't matter, because a new group of students will debate the meaning of the same film next year, also without conclusively settling anything.

What knowledge can be gleaned from language so sloppy that nobody can agree to its meaning? It's easy to cede that all writing is open to some degree of interpretation, but when does writing cross the line of being muddled and opaque to the point of uselessness? That line is demarcated by poetry. It's where communication goes to die. Like buying a yacht, it's completely impractical and only impresses fellow assholes.

Poetry doesn't enrich, it annoys. Pass.

FUCK YOUR
WEIGHT-LOSS INSECURITY

When people congratulate me for losing weight, I'm always confused. I didn't do it for myself, I did it to make them feel bad. When I monitor my caloric intake, exercise and control my portions to attain a healthy body-mass index, it's first and foremost a statement about other people's inadequacies. Great depictions of art and beautiful musical compositions are similarly meant to make you feel insecure about your own lack of talents and abilities. That's the inevitable conclusion one should draw from other people's achievements.

Losing weight is similar to topping a video game leaderboard: You aren't doing it to attain a personal sense of accomplishment. Who cares? You're doing it to make other players feel inferior.

Spite is an underrated motivator. After all, one of my goals with achieving success as a writer was to spite the people and organizations who doubted me along my path. Spite motivated me to strive for success in my professional career, and beyond. There's no reason why spite can't be equally motivating in other areas of life, such as education, employment, relationships and overcoming spite.

One of the best feelings in life is seeing an ex in a restaurant or bar while you're with a new, more attractive and more successful partner. Or when an employee clashes with his or her management over the direction to take on a project, nothing gives them that sweet hit of righteous indignation like achieving success on their own. There are two ways to look at the success of others: as a highlight of the things you lack, or as a challenge to step up your game.

When it comes to personal achievements, there's no shortage of jerks to inspire you to go after your pettiest dreams.

FUCK CHILDREN
(BUT DON'T)

Kids are underqualified adults. Every time a child threatens to run away from home, an adult's first response should be to chuckle and say "Go ahead, idiot!" That's because adults are awesome, and we know that kids are utterly useless death magnets who wouldn't survive more than a few hours on their own. Kids don't know how to cook, clean or even look out for danger properly. The most easily preventable form of death by crossing the street is to look both ways for cars, and yet children have to be constantly reminded to "look" with their eyes. All they have to do is keep their eyes open and turn their heads a little bit. That's it. It's the most preventable form of pedestrian death, and kids regularly fail this most basic of life skills.

Society is constantly bending over backward to safeguard these half-people. There are countless laws preventing kids from buying everything from alcohol, tobacco, fireworks, video games, spray paint and lotto tickets—as well as adult-themed movies, magazines and comics—all under the pretense that kids are idiots.

Kids have no concept of moderation when it comes to sweets, if child-protection laws are any indication. There are laws in the United States and Europe with restrictions on how advertisers can promote candy and food to kids because they are so suggestible.

There are also laws specifying when networks can air so-called adult-themed content, which includes programming with concepts that are difficult for a child to tackle, like war, drug use and suicide. Adult-themed content should be aired when kids are *more* likely to be awake, not less, because the main theme of adulthood is crippling depression and disappointment. You want your kids to be prepared for life? Show them what they're in for.

Children shouldn't be trusted with spray paint, not because adults are afraid they'll use it for graffiti—we know they will—but because kids are bad at spelling and grammar. The laws preventing the sale of spray paint should be literacy-based, not age-based. I don't want to see a poorly drawn tag on a train from some kid who thinks she's the "CHOOSEN ONE." Yeah, apparently not "choosen" for higher education, dumbass.

Laws preventing kids from gambling or buying lotto tickets are taken for granted, but rarely do people stop to ask: Why? It's easy to speculate that preventing children from buying lotto tickets is yet another safeguard to protect them from forming compulsive habits. But the real reason is that kids can't be trusted with money. I once took a kid shopping because his mom was a turbo-babe who got killed in an accident when she came to visit me while I was doing donuts on my motorcycle in my living room. As she handed me a crumpled twenty, her dying wish was for me to take her son shopping for whatever he wanted. So I took this kid to the store, and after hours of meandering up and down the aisles, the child settled on buying a giant hollow chocolate Easter egg, a pair of reading glasses that he didn't need and adult pullup diapers that actually did come in handy when I shit in them because doing so happened to be convenient. What a moron.

In 1952 the show *Art Linkletter's House Party* premiered on TV with a segment titled "Kids Say the Darndest Things." The word "darndest" is a folksy euphemism for "damnedest," which is still a more polite way of saying that kids say preposterous and idiotic things. The show was wildly popular and featured the host asking kids simple questions, like "What age would you like to get married?" or "Where would you like to go on your summer vacation?" And the child's response was always something stupid, like "Twelve" or "Heaven." The host's reaction was mild bemusement, and the audience laughed at the implications of a child wanting to die during his summer vacation. But the "joke" was always the same: Kids don't know shit. And in spite of this fact, adults constantly shield children from crucial information that will help them finally grow up. A little truth could be the salve that treats the epidemic of entitlement today's kids have. In the article "Is it bad to expose your kids to scary things,"[12] *Washington Post* editor Amy Joyce writes about tough questions her kids ask, like "Why doesn't Santa bring presents to homeless kids?" It's because some kids are poor, and Santa doesn't exist.

Kids don't ask for things, they demand them. The words "give me" are the most well-worn in a child's vocabulary. When a child isn't feeling particularly charitable, sometimes he or she won't even deign to grunt for what they want; they point. There have been emperors and tyrants throughout history who've had better manners than children. On the off chance a child wants to do something other than sponge off his parents, there are child-employment laws preventing children from working in coal mines. Children are the perfect size to crawl into hard-to-reach crevices in mine shafts, and their hands are ideal for polishing bullet casings during war, but the second you glance at a child's résumé—which is poorly written garbage anyway—Child Protective Services comes breathing down your neck.

Why do we have Child Protective Services? Aren't adults the ones who need protection? Adults are far more likely to die in bar brawls, gang rumbles with greasers, or fighting in global martial arts tournaments orchestrated by the Shadaloo syndicate. Isn't it about time we started caring for the caregivers?

When adults finally get fed up with a child's bullshit, there are even laws preventing them from leaving. The United Kingdom passed a law titled Children and Young Persons Act of 1933, which made it illegal to "abandon" any person under the age of sixteen. So if your child decides to be a sociopath and threatens you, steals your belongings, or you're just tired of his or her shitty attitude, too bad! You're stuck with that shithead for at least a decade and a half. Parliament made it illegal to abandon a child, not because it cares about the child's well-being so much as it doesn't want to be stuck with these horrible children either. Children suck so bad that societies pass laws so that even *they* don't have to look after your ugly kid. Fuck kids (but don't).

FUCK ONLINE REVIEWS

There are only five reasons to write online reviews, and none of them have any merit. The full implication is that we, as a society, are making decisions informed by the opinions of duplicitous people with dubious intentions. Here's a list of the reasons people write reviews, and why each reason is turd water:

Malice

One of the most common types of reviews people write are negative. These reviews are meant to hurt a business, enterprise, or personal reputation. Even when someone genuinely intends to warn others about a potential pitfall, this seemingly altruistic endeavor always has an element of spite associated with it.

Do we actually care about the plight of strangers? If you had a bad experience at a restaurant, is your intention first and foremost to warn a person you've never met? Why do you suddenly care so much about the customer-service experiences of people you don't know, when there are millions of people suffering all around the world whom you could be helping? Don't pretend like these reviews are for anyone but yourself. Being spiteful feels amazing, like you've righted a wrong done against you. It's a pettiness that temporarily fills the emptiness in your soul with rock salt.

A petulant response to a slight, real or perceived, speaks to a person's toxicity. Trusting a negative review is essentially putting yourself in the hands of a spiteful character in an emotional frame of mind. Anger is a fit of madness, so the experience being reported is dubious at best.

Fake Altruism

In its purest form, altruism is the unselfish concern for others. When it comes to online reviews, the case could be made that they may help future consumers make purchasing decisions. Spending time and energy writing a well-crafted review could be seen as a selfless act—*if* it were done anonymously. When it comes to charity, anonymity is the closest you can come to being completely selfless, short of committing suicide or receiving debilitating brain surgery immediately after your charitable act. To be truly selfless, one has to forgo all rewards, including the good feeling one gets from helping others. This feat can be accomplished only by killing yourself or rendering your mind incapable of remembering your altruistic deed.

Receiving credit for posting a popular review precludes the reviewer from claiming altruism as a motive. Reviews that are particularly well received, like those that are rewarded with "helpful" votes on popular online retailer sites like Amazon.com, give the reviewer a surge of euphoria. The validation one receives from the public is a powerful motivator to write reviews. There's the further possibility that your review may be particularly entertaining or well written, which opens the door for your review being shared by others, selected for publication and even going viral, all of which are highly selfish incentives.

Social Status

The mere act of writing a review on a product can elevate one's social status, especially if the product they are reviewing is expensive or popular. Writing a review of a luxury item is tantamount to telling people you're rich. It's a way of showing off your wealth without explicitly mentioning it, similar to wearing a band shirt from a foreign tour that you attended. Attending a play or musical on Broadway in New York is one of the most expensive pastimes in the United States, so simply sharing your opinion of a Broadway show is like stating your opinion of your luxury car's performance—irrelevant to most people and a showy inference to your wealth.

Even if the item you're reviewing isn't expensive, leaving a positive review on a product or business that's already viewed positively will signal to others that you have good taste, or you at least share a popular opinion. Even if the product is universally hated, negative reviews of products that everyone hates can raise your social standing with haters and may even influence others to write negative reviews that they otherwise wouldn't. I've even heard that one can make an entire career out of being negative on the Internet.

In the 1950s, a researcher named Solomon Asch conducted a series of experiments. He tested how likely people would be to conform to the beliefs of a group of collaborators to whom Asch knowingly gave a wrong answer to a simple test. One such test asked participants which line on the left side of a paper matched one of three lines on the right, where the three lines on the right were obviously distinct and easy to match. When the group of confederates chose the wrong answer, roughly a third of the participants who weren't in on the ruse gave the wrong answer to conform with the group.[13] This experiment came to be known as the "Asch Conformity Experiment" and may have implications in online reviews. People who glance at reviews that are either largely positive or negative ahead of writing their own reviews may be influenced by them, causing a conformity bias in their responses.

Vanity

When millions of people watch a video online and only two or three thousand people leave comments, clearly, commenting takes a certain mind-set that the majority of people don't have. That mind-set is narcissism. People who leave online comments on heavily trafficked forums usually have an exaggerated sense of self-worth. They're like a person at a concert shouting song requests at the band onstage, as if the band doesn't have a well-rehearsed set in mind that's expertly coordinated with lights and stage cues. People who leave comments on videos with millions of views think that their opinion is not only important enough to be read but noteworthy enough to warrant distinction from the thousands of other comments.

Having been a professional satirist for over two decades, I've received hundreds of thousands of emails from people from all walks of life. One of the most annoying categories is those from readers who feel slighted if I don't reply to them. Their inflated sense of self-importance is nauseating, and this is coming from a guy whose website is titled The Best Page in the Universe. I rarely email celebrities or people of note for the same reason: They're probably busy and don't have time to have a lengthy conversation with me. On the occasion that I do contact someone popular or important, the response I usually receive is a gift basket for my time, since there's no one more important than me. But if there's ever an occasion where someone doesn't reply, I don't react like I have a sandy vagina.

People write reviews for revenge, status, or their own amusement. The backbone of the referral industry is made up of these selfish, petty people. The best motive for an honest review may be money. A salaried journalist won't depend on kickbacks or perks from a manufacturer or restaurant owner. His or her paycheck would come from an unaffiliated source (his or her employer), and he or she would be so jaded to writing reviews that bias would be a nonfactor. He might even be an expert at what he's reviewing. Hell, we could coin a word for these writers and call them "journalists." What a concept! Instead, we have replaced journalists with John Q. Dipshit and his keyboard of justice.

FUCK DICHOTOMIES

One of the worst symptoms of flawed thinking is the false dichotomy fallacy. It's the belief that disliking something is an automatic support of the opposite. It's a red flag that signals to me that I'm about to engage in a tedious debate with a moron.

It's exhausting having to defend yourself against an implicit strawman argument being made every time you admonish someone or something. Don't like Marvel? You must be a fan of DC. Don't believe in God? You must be an atheist.

For example, criticizing a liberal candidate will lead these slow thinkers to believe you must be a conservative, or vice versa. The most obnoxious thing about this flawed thought process is that the idiot thinks you're the one who's an idiot.

For example, I've famously complained about Apple products, ever since the first iPhone debuted in 2007. The original model of the phone couldn't send picture messages, couldn't copy and paste, couldn't install any apps, had no customizable ringtones, no replaceable battery (still doesn't), no expandable storage (still doesn't) and the list goes on and on. In short, it was a technological travesty where even its sole "innovation," the touchscreen, was stolen from the LG Prada, a phone released a year before the iPhone. The iPhone's shortcomings are emblematic of Apple's philosophy as a company: form over function, to a fault. It seemed indisputable that the phone was abject garbage.

I wrote an article stating as much, which was hugely popular at the time and garnered over 6 million views. One common rebuttal I kept receiving over and over from the cult of Apple zealots was that I must be a fan of their competitor, Windows. The problem with this assumption is that I think Windows is also horse shit. Both companies seem to loathe their customers in different ways. Apple treats their customers like children, preventing them from opening the phone's hardware or even accessing any material they deem unsuitable in their app store. Windows puts about as much thought into user experience as an incontinent drunk puts into finding a place to pop a squat.

Microsoft may be the most successful global company to lack any semblance of vision. They ditch their own formula for success by releasing wildly different versions of their software that break backwards compatibility and change workflow shortcuts. They add bloat to every facet of the operating system, so nothing short of the most modern processors can run their software. It's a lose/lose situation, and my hatred of Apple products is in no way an endorsement of Microsoft's shitty offerings. My disdain for Apple also happens to be personal, since they've demonstrated terrible taste by blocking my website in their stores.*

False dichotomies make us choose between wanting our left eye or right eye poked out. This dichotomous thinking is reflected by the U.S. political system during every tedious multiyear election cycle. People can't seem to wrap their minds around an inde-

---

* Check for yourself: As of this writing, typing my web address, http://maddox .xmission.com, into a browser at an Apple store will redirect you to an advertisement for one of their products, which implies that I endorse Apple. I do not.

pendent candidate ever factoring into the national discussion. That's why we're often left choosing between two mediocre demagogues rather than an intellectual powerhouse like myself, who would solve all of the world's problems in minutes.

This problem likely stems from childhood, when parents offer children one of two choices at dinner: eat what's available, or eat nothing at all. Children are too stupid and weak to get their own jobs and buy and prepare their own dinners. That's why college is so enlightening to people: It's the first time in many people's lives that they realize there are other choices than starving or eating what your parents give you. For example, you can find a date to buy you a spaghetti dinner, or you can sneak into a wake and eat leftover funereal meats. For those with a bit of imagination, the options are limitless. You don't have to choose between two options, because the world doesn't have to be reduced to a binary toggle.

FUCK DOG LOVERS

Dogs are stupid animals that eat their own shit and laugh at corny jokes. In spite of this, dog owners are by far the most likely class of people to ascribe undue praise for how "smart" their pets are.

A dog can be tricked by pretending to throw a ball but instead keeping it in your hand. These are also the kinds of tricks that children, apes and plants fall for. Making dogs slightly more tolerable than children, there is no social stigma associated with tying them to trees. There's nothing a dog can offer that will ever impress me, up to and including their loyal companionship. Dogs are loyal to a fault, but only because dogs can't recognize bad behavior in humans or know to ostracize it. A dog can watch you commit infidelity in your bedroom and think, *Business as usual.* Not only would the dog be indifferent to your infidelity, it would sit there watching you like a lecher.

Everyone from dictators to serial killers have had dogs for pets, and those dogs were all loyal to them too (Fig. 11). Hitler had a dog, and that dog was loyal to Hitler. What a piece of shit. Not a good boy.

Hitler's dog was a German shepherd* named Blondi. If you

---

*   Presumably a purebred.

Fig. 11: Adolf Hitler and Eva Braun with their dogs,
(left to right) Stasi and Blondi. Who's a good boy?
Nobody. Nobody in this picture is a good boy.

visited your grandma's house and she had a German shepherd named Blondi, you might reduce yourself to using infantile language while you pet her and she wags her tail, all without realizing the dark truth: You are petting a Nazi.

I'm always wary of an animal's affection that's predicated upon you feeding it. A dog's loyalty can be bought. Dogs don't care about humans any more than ants care about aphids. All dog owners think they have a unique bond with their animals, but stop feeding a dog and see how quickly it will bite off and devour your face and the faces of everyone you've ever loved. A dog's affection can be bought by any human willing to give it a morsel of food. Dogs are not complicated in the same way that cars are not complicated: Put fuel inside it, and it will function how it's supposed to.

Dog Lovers Are Bullies

Dog lovers are hostile toward people who don't share their sentiments. It should be an inalienable human right to speak one's true opinion about how ugly any pet is. In an era when it's politically incorrect to print a denominational holiday greeting on coffee cups, criticizing an animal is one of the last frontiers of completely unfiltered thought. Yet we all feel silenced when we encounter dogs that look like fuzzy turd piles. Their zealot owners are completely infatuated with their dogs, to the point where they not only reject the notion that someone might not be equally infatuated but they become hostile toward dissenters. Dog owners will harangue you for daring to express your reasons for not being in love with their dogs, and every reasonable explanation is met with a haughty rebuttal:

"I don't like dogs, because they bite."

"Oh, not my dog, Blondi is a sweetheart."

Every dog is a "sweetheart" until it bites you. I've been told over half a dozen times in my life that a dog was a sweetheart and have been bitten by four of those dogs—and then the owners get uppity when you suggest the dog should be put down. If I had a robotic pet that I presented as "no threat to humans," but then every once in a while my robo-pet shaved a layer of skin off your ass with laser beams, you'd bet your shaved ass that people would want that robot to be put down. When that robot is a dog, everyone gets all weepy eyed. But remember, dogs are killing machines. Lasers are much less threatening than teeth. Would you rather your surgeon operate using lasers or using teeth?

When dogs aren't killing, they're shitting. Dogs are prolific shitters. In spite of what you've read up to this point in the chapter, I actually like dogs slightly more than I dislike them. However, I dislike carrying dog shit significantly more than I like dogs.

For that reason, I don't own one. There's a simple conditional statement for whether or not you should get a dog; each variable is to be assigned a value between 1 and 5, where 1 = not much and 5 = very much:

Q = How much you like dogs

P = How much you hate carrying dog shit

If P is greater than Q, then don't get a dog. It's that simple. My Q/P ratio is 2:5, by the way. Dogs shit everywhere all the time, and if they were even a fraction as smart as dog apologists say, they'd have learned by now that humans don't like their shit. Cats know to bury their shame like a teen hides his cum sock. Dogs will live with you for over a decade and never suspect how much their shit annoys you. In fact, dogs will shamelessly lock eyes with you while pinching off a hot pile of ass fudge. Some dog lovers selfishly leave the shit on the sidewalk, where people will step on it and have their weeks ruined. The amount of time I've spent trying to scrub excrement out of my shoes versus the amount of time I've spent enjoying a dog's company is criminal. Since I don't own a dog, the amount of time I *should* spend scrubbing shit is zero.

Dogs are lousy conversationalists. They answer questions with one of two responses: barking or panting like idiots.

Barking is a nuisance, but panting is downright creepy. It's a common misconception for children and morons to think that dogs pant because they're happy. Dogs pant because, like whales, they can't sweat. That means dogs always smell like a mixture of armpits, hockey equipment and car vomit. Their fur occasionally blankets their stink, but a light rain will reveal their true odorous nature. What's disconcerting about a dog's panting is that it's hard to tell whether a dog is dangerously overheated or not until it dies. Whenever I see a dog panting, I calmly back away and hope nobody notices, because I don't want to be responsible for disposing of its corpse. In addition to the small poop bags they carry, dog lovers should also carry around larger body bags, in case of fatal overheating. Of course, given their disheartening track record of leaving feces on sidewalks, dog lovers are likely to leave their dead bodies as well, leaving unwitting pedestrians with the task of having to scrape not just feces but entire corpses from their shoes.

There are countless videos online in which dog owners film their pets running into a window or doing something objectively stupid, like trying to carry a stick through a door frame that's too narrow. The dogs never understand why their owners are laughing at them. Dogs lack the self-awareness to realize the laughter is at their expense, as well as the self-esteem to care. Dog lovers don't love their dogs in spite of their stupidity but because of it. But that doesn't stop dog lovers from constantly reminding us that the same animal that chases its own tail has great levels of intelligence and empathy.

Dog lovers fancy themselves experts in canine psychology, but humans don't actually know what dogs are thinking because humans aren't dogs. Yet this truism doesn't stop people from projecting human emotions onto their pets. For example, a wagging tail is considered a sign of "happiness," but nobody knows why dogs wag their tails. Dog lovers will bloviate for hours about what a dog's tail wagging means, brushing aside the fact that it's difficult enough to even tell what another human is thinking, let alone another species. Two humans can stare at each other in a waiting room for hours and not know what the other is thinking. Yet at a mere glance, we're able to infer the emotional state of an entirely different species? We don't know when a dog is happy any more than we know when a dog is feeling optimistic, sincere, arrogant, or cheeky. When people anthropomorphize animals, they ascribe human emotions to what is in all likelihood involuntary or hereditary responses to the animal's environment. There's even some evidence that the direction of tail wagging is rooted in different hemispheres of a dog's brain.[14]

Every time I'm about to feed a dog a raw onion, the owner freaks out and reminds me that dogs can't eat them. I don't need to be reminded, I know. A dog will stare at you plaintively while you eat food that will kill it, like chocolate and onions, shamelessly begging for a morsel. It's like begging to eat buckshot.

When dogs finally find something they can eat that won't kill them, they start dripping gallons of slobber. It's high time we call it what it really is: a biohazard. I once had a friend who adopted a dog because he was in the mood to have a lifelong burden. My friend slipped on a puddle of slobber and broke every bone in his body, even his eardrums. I had to put my friend down, and nobody attended his funeral because they were too embarrassed to be associated with him. Dogs are killing machines, and dog lovers are idiots.

FUCK YOUR OBJECTION TO SEXUAL OBJECTIFICATION

Sexual objectification is bad only if you think sex is bad. Because sex is awesome, sexual objectification is awesome. Objectification is any interaction with a human being that is impersonal. It's treating another human being like an object. Why is that bad? People get objectified all the time. I walked into the post office a few weeks ago, went up to the clerk, handed her my package and left without saying a word. I used that teller as a shipping dispenser, which is essentially just a hole. I didn't say hello, learn her name, or ask how she was doing. I have no idea how many kids she might have or whether they were planned. I don't know what her favorite movies are and, frankly, I don't care. All I wanted to do was hand her my parcel and leave—and that's totally fine. People shouldn't be expected to chat with clerks when there's a long queue of people waiting to conduct their business. A busy post office isn't the place for idle conversation. The people behind you in line, as well as the clerk's supervisors, will thank you for abstaining from your polite but counterproductive conversations.

We have moments like this all the time. If you walk into a grocery store with automated checkout stands, you can use a machine to scan your groceries and ring you up. A machine is a literal object, so nobody will impugn you for treating it like one.

But what if you pay a cashier for your groceries and treat him or her like an automated checkout stand? Other than the cursory and optional greeting, you likely won't have a conversation with the clerk. He or she is, for all intents and purposes, a machine; you have objectified them. What if the customer doesn't speak English or is mute? Should we employ a Small Talk Inquisition to interrogate customers on whether they have a legitimate reason to abstain from chitchat?

Even if the customer does opt to have a conversation with the salesclerk, these conversations are often superficial and meaningless. The "hello"s and "how's it going"s disappear into the ether moments after they're uttered. The salesclerk's banter about the weather, or how the day has been going, is instantly forgotten, because we don't care. And if you're the type of person reading this thinking "But I do care! I ask those questions sincerely," you have a bigger problem at hand: self-deception. These micro-conversations are called "small talk" for a reason. The significance of these conversations is just that: small. If we need more evidence of the unimportance of small talk, observe the masses of customers who are barely glancing up from their phones to acknowledge the clerk. They are checked out while checking out and effectively dehumanizing the person with whom they're interacting. By not acknowledging someone who's doing something for you, you are quite literally treating them as a "thing" instead of a person.

When you hop on a bus and hop off without talking with the bus driver, there aren't droves of people reprimanding you for public transit objectification. You are expected to get on the bus, keep to yourself and refrain from disrupting the commute. In fact, chitchatting with the bus driver may distract him or her and jeopardize the lives of the other passengers.

If all of these forms of social objectification are okay, toler-ated and expected, then why is sexual objectification bad? If you use someone sexually, such as paying a woman or man for a sexually suggestive or explicit photoshoot, that's largely considered "sexual objectification," a phrase loaded with nega-tive connotations. Nobody ever says someone has been sexu-ally objectified in a good way. It's considered wrong because we view sex as bad. If that weren't the case, then sexual objec-tification would be just as innocuous as the other forms of objectification we tolerate. We have words like "slut," "tramp," "man whore," "pervert," "nympho," and "deviant" for people who enjoy sex and partake in it recreationally. There aren't as many negatively loaded words levied against people who enjoy other natural human inclinations, such as eating, sleeping, or exercising. If a performer is shown sleeping in an ad or movie, no one calls him or her a "somnolence object." People who eat food in TV shows aren't chastised for being "mastication objects." Sex is considered singularly degrading and sex work deplorable, whereas working for minimum wage in a grocery store, ringing up bologna for shoppers chatting on their cell phones, is considered dignified.

The problem with sexual objectification isn't the fact that people are being objectified, it's the perceived loss of dignity when engaging in sexual pursuits. If I lend my services to a construction company, I employ the use of my arms, legs, back and six-pack abs. But the second I put my penis in the cement mixer, every-one loses their minds. Want to hire a tall person to play on your basketball team? No problem. Want to hire a buxom woman for an underwear ad? Sexual objectification! And with that label, all conversation ends. There's no debate as to why it's wrong. Worst of all, this designation further demonizes sex.

The only way that a sexual service would result in the loss of dignity is if that service was nonconsensual. There's a name for nonconsensual sexual services: rape. That key difference of consent doesn't seem to stop critics from invoking a false equivalency and victim status.

Being an object—a useful object—is one of the highest things one can aspire to in life. It's far worse to not be needed than to be used. Could positive objectification lead to fresh concepts, like "more human" or even "more than human?" People who focus on things that dehumanize us rarely have the intellectual fortitude to consider what it means to humanize someone, let alone the existence of higher-level concepts like that of "extra-human."* Most people who aren't dipshits would agree that a person with a prosthetic limb is no less a person. If their enhancements not only fulfill their normal human function but surpass it in some way—be it extra strength, dexterity, focus, optic or sonic clarity, enhanced depth perception, et cetera—then it would be appropriate to suggest that these people have become extra-human—or better than human—by becoming partly, and literally, an object in some way. We think no less of people who enhance their bodies with wearable technologies like heart-rate monitors or music players to become extra-human. But women who augment their breasts or asses with implants are called "plastic" and "fake." It's only when the enhancement is sexual in nature that zealots call it dehumanizing.

Sexual qualities are still qualities. Just because people can appreciate each other for their sexual qualities doesn't mean we can't also value each other for nonsexual qualities. That'd be like

---

* It was a conscious decision not to use the phrase "superhuman" here to avoid comparisons to superheroes and other made-up Nickelodeon bullshit.

someone taking offense at a compliment about the color of their car (Fig. 12).

Fig. 12: Rev up your engines for outrage!

Humans are capable of valuing each other for more than one quality simultaneously. If we watch pornography created by consenting adults, we're using those adults for our sexual gratification and nothing else. Just like you wouldn't ask or care about a store clerk's personal life, you probably don't care much about the personal life of the porn stars you watch—and you shouldn't, stalker. The only difference is that there's a huge double standard when it comes to sex. Objectification is an unavoidable consequence of living in modern society. Even if we wanted to "humanize" a person by getting to know them on a personal level, we wouldn't have the time or ability to get to know everyone who makes our lives possible. If you took a few minutes out of your day to talk with everyone who provided a service for you, you wouldn't have time to do anything else. Between the coffee baristas who serve you, the clerks at a grocery store, tellers at a bank, cashiers at a theater, people who hold doors open for us, bellhops, engineers who design your electronic goods, child laborers who make your clothes and authors who write your books, there are literally hundreds if not thousands of people who make your life possible every day. We don't personalize any of these people. They are all there for us to use, and we care about them only for as long as it takes for us to get what we want from them.

Celebrities are another type of person we objectify. We use them for our entertainment every day without getting to know them personally. When you watch an actor or actress in a film or TV show, you are using them only for as long as you want to be entertained; and when you're done or bored, you simply turn them off. Their entire existence comes to an end the second we feel a tinge of boredom, all at the press of a button. You fall asleep while watching them, text while they're performing and have them on in the background during dinner. And nobody thinks it's bad or wrong. The only time anyone seems to give a shit about people being objectified is when they're performing sexual services.

There's arguably no aspect of humanity more human than our reproduction. Even if we wanted to avoid sexual objectification, critics of sexualized media don't give us a path toward achieving this goal. Short of an outright puritanical ban on any media servicing the human need for sex, or creepily reaching out to performers individually to personalize them, there's not much we can do to solve this alleged problem. It's a problem with no solution, which is perfect for people who are more interested in complaining than solving anything.

Even if we were to entertain the thought that sexual objectification is somehow bad, demeaning, or dehumanizing, it raises a number of important questions we need to consider:

1. Are there degrees of objectification? And if so, what degree of objectification, if any, is tolerable?

2. If people can be objectified, can the opposite be true? Can they also be humanized? And if so, what does it mean to humanize someone? Can someone be objectified and then humanized? Is the process reversible?

3. Can objects be humanized? If so, are there different degrees of humanization? Is the process of humanization also reversible? And if so, can we reach an equilibrium where a thing is equal parts humanized and objectified so that their nature is indistinguishable?

When considering these questions, it should immediately serve to illustrate how little thought critics have put into sexual objectification theory. Can someone be objectified only a little? How can we measure objectification? Is it an absolute condition that's either true or false? Let's consider the following illustrations (Fig. 13).

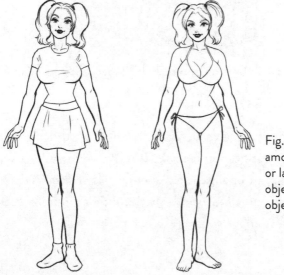

Fig. 13: Is the amount of clothing, or lack thereof, the objective measure of objectification?

Is the woman on the left less sexually objectified than the woman on the right? If so, by how much? And how can we compare sexual objectification metrics among different genders, ages and cultures?

What if we take the woman in the above illustration and dress her modestly? Has she now been humanized? And what about the reverse of sexual objectification? Can we take a sexual object, like a literal dildo, and humanize it (Fig. 14)?

Fig. 14: This regal dildo is a philanthropist, volunteer and pillar of the community.

These questions serve to demonstrate how absurd the criticism of sexual objectification really is. Just like you wouldn't start talking to a dildo just because it has a set of eyes and looks deeply contemplative, you wouldn't suddenly think that a human being was a literal object unless you were a sociopath.

FUCK YOUR SHITTY OPINIONS

Most people suck at writing and should shut up. Today, every idiot with a lame opinion is able to chime in with lightning speed and abject disregard for clarity. We've built the most sophisticated communications network the world has ever seen, with thousands of server farms hosting hundreds of thousands of servers, trillions of terabytes of storage and enough computing power to solve a Rubik's Cube the size of our sun. All we're doing with it is posting hackneyed political opinions and trite comments about topical news stories.

A good writer—one who can communicate his or her ideas with economical prose—practices for years in order to master the craft. Becoming an effective writer requires research, hard work and a strong point of view. Writing is easy, but communicating effectively is hard.

You wouldn't go to your mechanic for artwork, so why would you go to your aunt or grade-school friend for social commentary? You think writers just wake up one day and are able to spit out brilliant prose? It requires decades of hair-pulling frustration, grueling deadlines and enough coffee to dissolve a corpse. Good writing takes experience and discipline that most people don't have. And "most people" is the group that makes up your social news feeds. These are the people who choose to while away their time with their families, careers and social obligations. They're safe, nice and normal people who live safe, nice and normal lives. These aren't the people who are furthering political discourse with their paradigm-shifting narratives. They're simple people toeing the line with platitudes.

Based on a lifetime's experience eating mediocre potato salad at backyard potlucks, I've concluded that most people are casual cooks at best. We wouldn't turn to them for culinary expertise beyond toast and various boiled noodles bullshit. So why are we resigning ourselves to the half-baked social commentary of casual writers? The speed and ease with which social networking has allowed people to post their inane opinions has lowered the quality of discourse. The writing you see in magazines, newspapers, or books has been toiled upon for hours. It will have gone through multiple drafts, structural revisions and edits. By the time you see it, a published piece will have survived the unmerciful cuts of editors, copyeditors, fact-checkers and proofreaders. Published writing is like the one triumphant sperm that reaches your ocular ovaries. This revision process produces the best writing. It's the greatest sign of respect that you can demonstrate to a reader. You care enough about your writing to show them only what they need to see, in order to communicate your ideas to them. The unspoken message is that you appreciate the reader's time.

Posts on social networks, on the other hand, are entirely disposable. Further, this seemingly harmless act of sharing our inane lives with our friends potentially carries disastrous consequences. One of the most important aspects of our identity is our reputation, which can be dashed in seconds by posting a careless thought or unrefined opinion. In 2013 Justine Sacco, the senior director of corporate communications at IAC, a U.S.-based Internet and media company in charge of dozens of large websites such as OkCupid, CollegeHumor and Dictionary.com, sent off a tweet just before boarding a flight to Cape Town, South Africa, saying "Going to Africa. Hope I don't get AIDS. Just kidding. I'm white!" It was a dark bit of sarcasm that can be viewed as a statement about how most people fortunate enough to be born in a wealthy, predominantly white country never have to worry about the ravages of a disease that has crippled poorer, mostly African countries. It wasn't particularly funny or poignant, but it's exactly the type of thoughtless joke people post online regularly.[15]

She thought nothing of the tweet and boarded her flight. When she landed, she turned on her phone to a deluge of texts from her friends telling her that her tweet had been spread and that she'd become a trending story on Twitter. Her feed was flooded with angry messages from people calling her tweet racist, ignorant and offensive. Her employer decided to terminate her, and the world knew about it before her plane had even landed. She spent the better part of the following year and a half battling depression and trying to salvage her reputation online, which is difficult to do in a digital age when nothing is ever erased and our permanent reputations are one Google click away. This type of social media self-destruction is becoming far too common and can happen to any of us without the proper care and attention to our writing. We're all one sentence away from ruining our lives, and people still post their inane thoughts flippantly.

When you type into the input field on a social networking site, you will get, at most, a red underline if you misspell a word. You don't get the feedback of an experienced editor or a second set of eyes reading your writing. That little red underline is as close as most people will ever come to having their writing scrutinized for quality before it's irrevocably published for a global audience. The business models of social networking sites are not aligned with the goal of improving discourse, and a carefully worded post may be less profitable for them for two reasons.

First, as illustrated in the Sacco case, these types of social media meltdowns cause a flurry of online activity. The social media business model is rewarded by traffic spikes. The activity gets packaged in impressive reports that are then presented to advertisers to justify higher ad rates. They couldn't care less that the activity is due to people's lives being destroyed or that it comes at the expense of public discourse being dumbed down. It's a good story, and good stories drive traffic. The torch-and-pitchfork-wielding Internet mob loves to impugn people for perceived slights, and social networking makes it easy.

Second, every status update you post is an opportunity for their servers to poll your writing for keywords to serve you targeted ads. It's in their best interests to get you to post quickly and frequently. The less thought you put into the post, the easier it is for a computer to categorize your statement algorithmically. The more spontaneous your posts are, the less likely your writing will include a rich vocabulary or a nuanced opinion that's difficult for computers to quantify. Computers can interpret a simple statement about how you feel with a high degree of accuracy based on a large sample of similarly worded statements other people have made. To that end, they've made it even easier to communicate what you're feeling by reducing it to one emoji character to illustrate your emotions. Social networks can map complex emotional states to individual characters, which makes it easier for them to pair up ads for the right emotion you're feeling.

Feeling sad? Why not express yourself with a frowny-face emoji? Social networks can keep tabs on your emotional state, and if you tend to post too many "sad words"* you might be depressed and it would be profitable for the manufacturer of an antidepressant drug to know that. Going on many first-dates? Well, there are some hot singles in your area that you might be interested in. Social networks aren't interested in long posts describing first dates in detail. The longer your post is, the harder it will be to pigeonhole and then serve ads to you based on your interests. If you write a sentence about going on a date, it's computationally trivial to infer that the subject of your post is dating. If you write a page about going on a date where you got a flat tire, went out to dinner, met some friends, talked about politics and saw a movie, it broadens the number of keywords that ad-servers can poll to determine which ads to serve to you. Are you interested in tires? Food? Politics? Movies? The focus becomes obfuscated and your post less valuable.

So what's the solution? Shut up. If you aren't good at expressing yourself, then stop doing it publicly. That's why people used to keep journals and diaries hidden under their beds; they're too embarrassing for anyone else to read. If you don't spend hours writing every week, you are in all likelihood a shitty writer. Hell, even if you do, you're probably a shitty writer. Spare us your literary diarrhea. Whatever opinions you have about whatever topical story you want to chime in on have probably already been expressed more coherently by someone else. That doesn't mean you should quit trying to express yourself entirely, but you should put extra thought and care into what you post online. Not every photo, thought, or utterance has to be shared. You're not that important.

---

* Words can be cross-referenced with tables that correspond to emotional values, so a list of "sad words" might include "depressed," "angry," "loss," "grief," "unemployed," "frustrated," et cetera.

FUCK BEING OFFENDED

Being offended is a choice. The offense begins, persists and terminates entirely in your mind. The power to offend does not exist, and offense isn't something we can wield like a weapon against other people. It is always a decision that is made by the person taking offense.

The best evidence for this assertion is the fact that people can get offended by objects. For example, there's a fountain in Switzerland called "Child Eater" (Fig. 15). The statue was created in the mid-1500s by Swiss sculptor Hans Gieng, who depicted an ogre eating a child, with a bag full of more children at his side (for later). People have speculated about its meaning and awesomeness, yet many find it objectionable. It turns out that parents are especially squeamish when it comes to depictions of children being cannibalized. As a person who has no children, this sculpture doesn't bother me at all. In fact, I prefer it to other sculptures. I intend to print out and carry with me a wallet-sized photo of this sculpture in place of the children I don't have. I'd love to have a replica of this sculpture as a hood ornament, to let people know I'm stylish and mean business.

In spite of the fact that this is an inanimate object, the creator of which has long since passed away, people still take offense to it.

Fig. 15:
Kindlifresserbrunnen
(Child Eater Fountain).

Gieng couldn't have known that, centuries after creating this masterpiece, people he'd never met from all around the world would be repulsed by his humble portrayal of an ogre enjoying a hearty sack of children. If you are personally offended by this sculpture, it isn't Gieng's intent—his body had completely decomposed before your birth.

It's trivial to demonstrate that offense is received rather than given, because people can even take offense to "vulgar" formations in nature, like the so-called Fairy Chimneys in Cappadocia, Turkey, which look like giant stone boners (Fig. 16). These formations are a natural reminder that even Mother Earth can offend people who have modest cock sensibilities. No human is to blame for the phallic appearance of these pillars or any offense they may cause, so the entire onus is on the viewer, who should really get a grip.

Fig. 16: Cappadocia, Turkey, home of nature's boner.

Nothing is "universally offensive." Literally every single offense a person might take, or social taboo we might have, is a choice that individual has made. The choice to be offended is about the person being offended, not the person making the alleged offense. For example, here's a matrix of groups along with a partial list of things that offend them:

TABLE 1

Offended Group:	Offended By:
Parents	• Criticism of, or advice about, child-rearing • Sexual or adult themes in TV, movies, or video games • Violence in the media • Statues of ogres eating children • "Foul" language • Drug marketing

Offended Group:	Offended By:
Feminists	• Criticism of, or advice about, feminism • Sexual themes in TV, movies and video games • Perceived "sexual objectification" • Catcalling • Rape jokes • Photoshopped magazine covers • Gender roles • Gendered language
Fat people	• Fat jokes • Fat shaming • Criticism of their looks • Suggestions to lose weight • Lack of fat accommodation • Lack of fat acceptance
Asexuals	• The suggestion that everyone enjoys or requires sex • The suggestion that there may be something cognitively or physiologically wrong with them • A lack of awareness of asexuality
Handicapped	• Jokes at their expense • Suggestions that they are less capable, either explicitly or tacitly, when people do things for them • A lack of understanding or consideration of their needs

Offended Group:	Offended By:
Transsexual people	• Intolerance of their lifestyles • Intrusive questions about their sex or genitalia • Doubt about their gender or sexual orientation • Jokes at their expense • Pejoratives like "tranny"
Black people	• Negative black stereotypes • A lack of understanding of challenges that are unique to black people • Suspicion or fear of black people • Racist slurs
Conservatives	• Flag burning • Abortion • Nontraditional marriage • Governmental oversight of businesses and personal property • People who don't recognize religious holidays or traditions
Liberals	• Politically incorrect terms • Insensitivity to racism, sexism, et cetera • Governmental oversight of recreational drugs and personal health decisions • Government endorsement of religion • People who don't recycle

Offended Group:	Offended By:
Atheists	• People who believe in deities • Any suggestion that they should believe in deities • The suggestion that atheists are not as ethical as religious people • Prayer as a force of change
Homosexuals	• The belief that homosexuality is wrong • Gay slurs • Gay stereotypes
Women	• The suggestion that women are physically weak or cognitively inferior • The expectation of traditional roles or duties (i.e., cooking, cleaning, housewife, mother, et cetera) • Excessive or exclusive sexual value at the expense of their other skills or talents
Men	• The suggestion that men are weak or effeminate • Emasculating insults • The expression of emotions • The suggestion that men are privileged • The inability to get laid • Questions of sexual virility

Offended Group:	Offended By:
White people	• Implied or explicit accusations of racism • The belief that white people have an automatic and unfair advantage in life for being white and the suggestion that white people haven't earned their wealth or social status • Real or perceived bias toward hiring minorities

This list is unexhausted and inconclusive, as there are many more groups of people with countless social taboos, ripe for offending. Many of these groups may overlap in the offenses they take, but the thing all these offenses have in common is that the person taking the offense has to make that decision for him- or herself. There's nothing physically different between a conservative and a liberal, so any offense each group might take is entirely arbitrary and based on a choice.

One of the biggest offenses that can be committed in public is the use of certain "obscene" or "vulgar" words. For example, if someone says the word "fuck" in conversation, it may offend the lesser mind who ascribes feelings of shame or angst to the word. A genius like myself would hear that word and treat it as a bit of spice peppered throughout an otherwise dull conversation that is the linguistic equivalent of hospital food. There's nothing inherently wrong with the word, or even the act to which it's referring. The words we utter are ultimately just sounds we make, except we've all decided that a grunt that starts with the sound of a hard "F" and ends with a sharp "k" is one we shouldn't say in polite company. People who don't want to be offended by this sound choose not to be. Good for them. They are the seed carriers; they are the ones who'll spread our genes after the apocalypse. Our alien or robotic overlords will be less than sympathetic to our linguistic sensitivities.

For every social taboo or offense one could take, it's trivial to find a person or group who doesn't take offense to it. For example, in the United States and much of the world, it's considered rude to ask someone how much money they make. However, this taboo is almost nonexistent among one-seventh of the world's population: the Chinese. Chinese people not only don't consider it rude to ask someone how much money they make, but also it's often one of the first questions asked when getting to know someone. It's as common as asking someone where they live or where they're from. In the United States, it's one of the few questions on surveys that consistently allow the "prefer not to say" option. In the United States, asking someone how much they make is a precursor to an awkward, stammering conversation if not outright refusal or hostility. Why is it so taboo? Who cares? And yet it's considered extremely rude to discuss divorce, death, or political issues in China, while people in America often talk about these issues openly. I've had very personal conversations with friends who've told me about abortions, marital infidelity and family infighting. Yet when the topic of money comes up, they get squeamish.

In spite of people's reluctance to discuss finances, we know roughly how well off a segment of the population is every time we see someone driving a high-end luxury vehicle. If the reason you don't discuss your income is to avoid appearing boastful if you're well off, then isn't the luxury car showing your hand, shithead? Not only is it false modesty to avoid discussing how much you make while driving a luxury car, but it's also even worse than having boasted in the first place, because in addition to boasting, now you're trying to seem virtuous for giving the false appearance of not boasting. Some people don't discuss income to avoid being judged by others, but rather than assuming that judgment by our peers will be a foregone conclusion, we could each simply choose not to judge others. Boom. I just solved the problem in one sentence. You're welcome.

Not only is the decision to take offense arbitrary, it's mentally exhausting and counterproductive. The time required to take offense, feel upset and then come down from the feelings of butthurt is time you could have spent doing anything else with your life. I posit the theory that being a victim makes people feel good. It evokes a childlike need for attention and care, much like how a mother kissing a scraped knee makes the child feel good. Children are idiots, and they think there are therapeutic properties to a mother's kiss. On the contrary, that kiss may even transmit bacteria into the open wound, causing the child to die. I always encourage parents to kiss their children's open wounds, and they think I'm being sweet. Fools.

When evaluating people for mental stability, a quick rule of thumb is to count the number of things they're offended by: If the number is greater than five, they are too sensitive and most likely emotional powder kegs. Every offense they take beyond the fifth increases precipitously the likelihood that the person will cry during any given hour. The number five isn't entirely arbitrary. The large list of groups with their corresponding offenses in Table 1 is a good starting point for how many offenses a person could feasibly take, as most people will belong to only one or two of the groups at any given time. Though it's possible for someone to be both black and gay for example, the likelihood of these overlaps occurring diminishes with the respective populations of each group.

Imagine a world in which a new breed of protohuman was born with a clean slate and no preconceived societal notions about what is or isn't considered offensive. Left to his or her own devices, it's reasonable to assume that this child wouldn't be offended by anything. A slur has no meaning without historical or social context. People who are offended by racial or sexist slurs are likely offended because the slurs themselves invoke an instance of discrimination, which is a real-world phenomenon, as opposed to purely psychological. The offense one takes is likely associated with the real injustice experienced by people who've been discriminated against. But without that empirical knowledge of discrimination, the new protohuman would be tough as nails and impervious to slurs. Or at the very least oblivious to them.

Nobody can make you feel anything with their words alone, unless you cede that power to them. Nothing is universally offensive, just as nothing is universally scary. Your reaction depends on your upbringing and life experiences. The easiest way not to be a victim is to decline the opportunity.

FUCK ABSTRACTION

Want to solve a specific problem? Then stop turning your specific problem into an abstract one. This chapter is dedicated to the brave men and women who've fought valiantly in all our generation's greatest wars since World War II: the War on Christmas, the War on Drugs, the War on Women, the War on Poverty, the War on Gangs and the War on Graffiti. Not to mention the War on Terror, which should be wrapping any day now, as soon as allied nations kill or capture every last thing that might instill terror in a populace.

People who take specific problems and try to make them abstract obfuscate the issues, making them impossible to solve. For example, some Christians want people to recognize their customs and traditions, such as store clerks greeting them with "Merry Christmas" instead of the more neutral "Happy Holidays." They will use the abstract concept of a metaphorical war being fought with imaginary agents, using rhetorical munitions and with unknown goals. U.S. conservatives started popularizing the phrase "War on Christmas" in the early 2000s. The fervor reached fever pitch in 2002 when a public school in New York banned nativity decorations for being overtly religious, while allowing so-called secular holiday decorations, such as Christmas trees. Who's fighting this war? Can it be won? What's the exit strategy? We'll probably never see the satisfying headline declaring that the "War on Christmas" is over because there are no metrics for victory. Nobody is keeping tally of the number of times store clerks say "Merry Christmas." Even if they were, what quota would constitute "mission accomplished"? It's just another opportunity to claim victimization.

Similarly, feminists often use the abstract concept of a "patriarchy" as the source of many of the world's problems. A patriarchy is a societal or governmental hierarchy in which men control the power. Never mind the fact that no true patriarchy exists in any modern Western civilization, as women currently hold or have held power in every major branch of government and corporate management. The ambiguous concept of male power still persists as a specter over many social ills in this world. The problem with using this concept in any meaningful way is that, again, there are no metrics of success or failure. If a patriarchy was purely a numerical consideration, one might conclude that a senate made of equal parts men and women would be purely egalitarian. However, it's trivial to demonstrate the numerical argument as being false.

Simply having women present doesn't guarantee that they will represent women's interests, any more than the presence of men will guarantee that they will represent male interests. After all, patriarchal power structures existed long before women's suffrage, and at some point the majority of men in a literal patriarchy ceded their power not just to women but other political minorities. It's common to find instances of men pushing for legislation in favor of women's interests. For example, in 2014, President Obama signed into law legislation like Executive Order 13655, which encourages wage transparency to combat real or perceived wage discrimination.[16] The entire premise of a representative government is that its members are representative of all their constituents, not just ones with whom they share the same skin color, ethnicity or genitals.

The phrase "war on" hit peak popularity between 2004 and 2006, due in no small part to the phrase "the war on terror" (Fig. 17).

Its shelf life was greatly diminished due to its overuse during those few years, causing "war on" to become stale. Pundits needed a new sexy phrase to spearhead their cause-du-jour, and "culture of" became the chosen expression to sate their appetite for abstraction. We are living in a "culture of shame," a "culture of fear," and a "culture of greed." In our culture of culture blaming, there's no such thing as independent events. Instead of discussing individual instances of animal abuse, we are now allegedly in a "culture of animal cruelty." Individual cases of sexual assault are no longer the problem, the real culprit is a "rape culture." Gun violence isn't a series of unfortunate events by troubled individuals, but we now live in a culture that permits and encourages gun violence. The phrase "culture of" has become the new "war on" (Fig. 18).

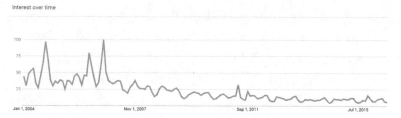

Fig. 17: Google Trends search for "the war on terror."

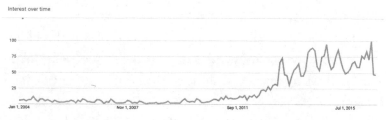

Fig. 18: Google Trends search for "rape culture."

Using the concept of a "culture" to attrbute blame is vague and abstract enough to describe everyone and no one simultaneously. It's the perfect phrase for politicians and advocacy groups, because they can use it to draw attention to their cause or issue— which they feel is so urgent and far reaching that it requires casting a net large enough to encompass every person on Earth. That's urgency to bank on.

Beyond the lazy rhetoric of culture blaming, the problem with turning concrete, quantifiable problems into abstract ones like "culture" is that the solution—cultural transformation—may be impossible. First, how do you even know with any degree of certainty that culture is the culprit to begin with? What conditions would need to be met before one can say with a high degree of certainty that it is definitely culture, and not the individual, that's the cause of a problem? And if we were to deduce with certainty that culture was the problem, cultural shifts usually happen a few times per decade at most, and no one person, organization, or government can steer them with any degree of control. Otherwise they would be doing it all the time.

There's no clear set of instructions for intentionally changing society at large. When we step back for a moment to assess what's being asked of us, the goal is Herculean: to change the minds, habits and opinions of hundreds of millions, if not billions, of individuals. And that's assuming "culture" is to blame in the first place, which, again, is hard to prove objectively.

The use of "rape culture" is a good example of why this obfuscation not only doesn't work, but sometimes does more harm than good. Many anti-sexual abuse activists blame sexual assault on a culture that is permissive and encouraging of sexual assault. The encouragement comes by way of glorified sexual violence, rape jokes and skepticism of sexual abuse claims in the media and pop culture.

The largest anti-sexual violence organization in the United States is RAINN: the Rape, Abuse & Incest National Network, which has openly decried the use of this phrase. RAINN states that the phrase shifts the onus of responsibility from the individual committing the offense to an abstract cultural element. The organization, which was founded in 1994 and exists to help victims of sexual abuse, surprised many anti-sexual abuse advocates when it made a public statement about the concept in 2014:

> *In the last few years, there has been an unfortunate trend towards blaming "rape culture" for the extensive problem of sexual violence on campuses. While it is helpful to point out the systemic barriers to addressing the problem, it is important to not lose sight of a simple fact: Rape is caused not by cultural factors but by the conscious decisions, of a small percentage of the community, to commit a violent crime.*[17]

This point was largely lost on the masses of well-intentioned idiots parroting what they'd read in political blogs, magazines and think pieces. In an article titled "Ten Things to End Rape Culture" published by *The Nation*, a piece "conceived by" Walter Moseley and "edited by" Rae Gomes suggest that "rape culture exists because we don't believe it does."[18] It's an assertion lifted right from the pages of *Peter Pan*. If we accept the premise that rape culture exists—we just need enough boys and girls to believe in it hard enough, and it will be magically wished out of existence! This is what passes for contemporary activism. The authors argue that the problem is "violent masculinity," suggesting that it's a problem so pervasive that it's "endemic," while simultaneously suggesting that "rape is not a normal or natural masculine urge." So which is it? How can the abstraction of violent masculinity be so pervasive as to be endemic, yet not be so pervasive that it's the norm? Those two precepts are mutually exclusive.

"Sexual violence is a pervasive problem," says the article, which "cannot be solved by analyzing individual situations," and violence isn't committed by individuals or groups of "crazies." This assertion is made without a shred of evidence. There's no reason an instance of sexual violence can't be "solved" by analyzing individual situations. Society has developed tools to handle violent individuals, such as cops, courts, prison, anger management counseling, SWAT teams and Chuck Norris. The article's assertions also directly contradict RAINN's own recommendations:

> . . . an inclination to focus on particular segments of the student population (e.g., athletes) . . . or traits that are common in many millions of law-abiding Americans (e.g., "masculinity"), rather than on the subpopulation at fault: those who choose to commit rape. This trend has the paradoxical effect of making it harder to stop sexual violence, since it removes the focus from the individual at fault, and seemingly mitigates personal responsibility for his or her own actions.

Making a tangible problem abstract makes it difficult, if not impossible, to solve. If you're trying to drive a nail, you use a hammer. You don't launch a social media campaign to raise awareness about the culture of protruding nails.

FUCK YOUR RACIST WITCH HUNT

If you have to label someone an extremist, they aren't one. Extremists aren't shy, coyly dancing around their ideologies until the moment you bravely call them out. Their beliefs are extreme—by definition—which means two things:

1. They can't shut the fuck up about them, and

2. They only have one switch: ON.

Extremists don't object to "the adulteration of Islam by the radicals who foment terrorism." They want to "Turn the Middle East to glass, God bless America, hot dogs with bacon, amen!"

There's an annoying trend on the Internet to label people in debates as racists, sexists or homophobes. The script plays out the same every time: Someone makes a comment that's perceived to be insensitive to an ethnic group, gender or sexual orientation, so the offended party jumps to the conclusion that the offender is an extremist.

Naturally, the offender denies being racist, sexist or homophobic, which should defeat the accusation right there. When people who are accused of having an extreme point of view find it completely objectionable to be aligned with those who actually share that viewpoint, it's unlikely that they are, in fact, fans of that ideology.

Racists, for example, wave around Confederate flags or yell "LOVE IT OR LEAVE IT!" They don't tiptoe around the Internet dropping subtle clues for chatroom detectives to piece together. They're posting unrepentant status updates about their inane political views and linking to conspiracy websites. They aren't interested in debating anyone about anything. They don't care about offending moderates because none of their friends are moderate. They've alienated themselves with their extreme opinions.

For example, if someone holds the sincere belief—no matter how unqualified their opinion may be—that a child is best raised by heterosexual couples, it doesn't automatically make them gay-hating bigots. Case in point, a man made headlines in 2015 when he suggested that a child should be born "naturally," without the aid of in vitro fertilization (IVF) and to a "traditional" family, consisting of a father and a mother. People called him homophobic.[19] This assertion was ridiculous, because the man who made these statements was the gay fashion designer Domenico Dolce, of Dolce & Gabbana fame. His statements were taken somewhat out of context from an interview with Italian magazine *Panorama*:[20]

> *"I am gay, I cannot have a child. I believe that we cannot have everything in life . . . it is also good to deprive yourself of [some things]. Life has its own natural course, there are things that must not be changed. And one of these is the family."*

Celebrities like Elton John fired off an angry volley of criticism, taking offense at Dolce's assertion that an IVF child was "synthetic."[21] Children born via IVF procedures have long been called "test tube babies," since the technique's very inception in 1978.[22] While it's understandable why parents of IVF children like Elton John would be sensitive to the pejoratives "test tube baby" or "synthetic," Dolce is hardly a frothing-at-the-mouth homophobe. As a gay man, he loves homosexuals very literally.

In context, his statements sound like a support of asceticism and self-denial as a virtue. Ascetics believe that abstaining from some worldly desires can lead to spiritual enlightenment. Almost every major religion in the world has a component of asceticism. For example, some Buddhists believe in acquiring only basic necessities, such as food, water, clothing and shelter, so that adherents can focus on meditation and spiritual enlightenment. Christianity, on the other hand, promotes a lesser degree of asceticism in the form of premarital abstinence—which is a shitty approach, if teen pregnancy rates are any indicator, and they are. Dolce's comment was a variation of the colloquialism that "You can't have your cake and eat it too." He's of the belief that people who can't have biological children shouldn't have them. While it's easy to build a rebuttal against this philosophy, it's not qualitatively equivalent to saying "I hate homosexuals." It's not even in the same ballpark. The ballpark isn't even in the same zip code. In fact, it's two towns over, and it's actually a burger stand.

Gone are the days of moderation in language. If someone says something that can be perceived as "sexist," he or she is no longer simply a sexist but a misogynist or misandrist—the most extreme forms of hate toward a gender. Calling someone a misogynist isn't equivalent to calling someone sexist. In fact, calling someone who makes a sexist statement "sexist" is making a huge assumption and ignoring a lot of granularity. Almost everyone has said or thought a sexist statement, both men and women alike. But saying an occasional sexist comment doesn't warrant labeling a person's sum identity as sexist. It's akin to calling someone who once changed a tire a "mechanic." Individual instances of a certain kind of behavior are exceptions to the rule, until we've observed multiple instances or an extreme type of that behavior. Only then are we justified in defining that behavior as part of a person's identity. And we usually don't have to look hard for clues.

Ever see a hippie banging drums in a park and feel the need to alert others that he or she is, in fact, a hippie? Of course not, because people have eyes, ears and the ability to smell patchouli and body funk. The act of looking for clues of a certain type of identity is itself annoying and counterproductive to a debate or conversation. Usually the reason people look for clues of another person's alleged racism is only so they can label them and dismiss their opinions outright. Labels serve to end conversations by stereotyping people. It's much easier to disregard what someone has to say by assuming that you already know everything that he or she has to say. It's the tactic of disingenuous people who are more interested in pious castigation than in debating their opinions in earnest.

I myself have been the subject of some of these labels. For example, when my first book, *The Alphabet of Manliness*, came out in 2006, it was almost universally praised and heralded for ushering in a new wave of male-centered humor lit that was almost nonexistent at the time. Prior to my book, only a handful of books had ever tackled the same demographic, and most of them included stereotypically masculine interests such as beer and fast cars. My writing, on the other hand, featured video games, hot sauce and lumberjacks prominently, without so much as the word "beer" even appearing in the manuscript. It was a brilliant approach by a brilliant writer, targeting other contemporary men. The book tapped into the zeitgeist and spawned dozens of pale imitations. The praise wasn't universal, however.

One of the critiques I received came from a pointed article written by some haughty blogger who accused me of being a "misogynist." Prior to my book, I'd only published a handful of articles about women on my site—which contained over three hundred written pages at the time, none of which espoused any hatred toward them. Her accusations were levied against me even though two of the illustrators I hired for my book were female. Even though I partnered up with a female illustrator for my comic book. Even though a small army of women were responsible for my book's publication. None of this matters, apparently, because if you make a joke that someone finds sexist, even once, you are a sexist for life. And not just a sexist, but a misogynist—the most extreme kind of sexist: a person who *hates* women.

If there's any prevailing characteristic of my writing and personality, it's that my opinions are loud, outspoken and always right. If I had the belief that women were inferior, I wouldn't dance around it and write a bunch of jokes in a book that's clearly satirical. People with strong or extreme opinions are usually bold and unafraid to voice them. We don't need hate detectives to suss out their "real" opinions.

FUCK BEING PROUD
OF WHO YOU ARE

Being proud of who you are is lazy self-affirmation for the unaccomplished. It's unearned praise that stems from a narrative your parents told you and exists separate from any outward personal achievements. This form of pride often includes personal traits we have no control over, such as our nationality, ethnicity, gender and even language.

Most patriotic people actually feel a sense of entitlement to the land they were born on, simply for being squirted there out from someone's vagina. Of all the things to feel entitled about, the choice of your parents to drunkenly conceive a child in a country they didn't have the gumption or ability to leave is at the bottom.

You were carried around in someone's ball sac with no cognizance of the world outside you. You didn't know your ancestry or what your parents may or may not have done to "fight" for your right to be in the country you were born in. Let's face it: Most people aren't great. Odds are your parents were very average, because most people are average, and that likely includes you.

We're told heroic tales of how our ancestors, collectively, fought for this land with their blood. But *your* ancestors probably didn't. Take the United States, for example. The population of the United States is about 320 million people as of this writing. The white colonial population in the United States during much of the 1700s was under 1 million people.[23] Of those, how many were accomplished statesmen or displayed great feats of heroism? If our history books are any indication—and they are, because they're history books—only a handful. Far fewer than 1 percent, because otherwise we'd have to memorize about 10,000 or so names in our textbooks. The truly notable early settlers and "founding fathers" numbered in the dozens, if that.

It's a probabilistic certainty that almost none of us are direct descendants from anyone great, and even if we are, that doesn't ensure that we won't be fuckups. Mozart's sons Karl and Franz Xaver Mozart didn't possess their father's seemingly innate musical ability, and they lived their lives in his shadow. They opted not to have children of their own, thus ending the Mozart lineage in one big disappointing whimper.

You haven't earned the pride you have in your heritage any more than you earned the food you were fed when you were born. Someone gave you a handout, and you accepted it like a needy loser. You aren't great just because someone great bore you, and your sense of pride in what your forefathers accomplished is unearned. You were born in a hospital that men greater than you built, and you were raised in a house that someone better than you bought and paid for. Your net contribution to the equation wasn't even enough to put you at zero. You were less than zero because you were dependent. You were born. That's it. Get over yourself. Identity isn't inherited, it's earned. Fuck being proud of who you are. Get to work.

FUCK FOLLOWING YOUR DREAMS

Everyone always tells you to follow your dreams, but rarely do we stop to ask: Why? People's dreams aren't always good, noble, or virtuous. Some people dream of exacting revenge upon someone who has slighted them, rekindling a toxic relationship, or committing grand larceny. From winning the lottery to prevailing in a frivolous lawsuit, our dreams aren't always productive or righteous. Many are fit for a supervillain. The belief that we should follow our dreams is a stupid, simplistic mantra that lacks foresight and introspection. Messages with positive intentions can resonate with people who have bad intentions too. Imagine if the leader of a rogue nation like North Korea followed his dream to reduce his enemies to seas of "flames and ash."[24]

Until they're acted upon, dreams are just fantasies. Many of the most lethal school shootings in the United States started out as the shooter's revenge fantasy. The Columbine shooters, for example, had an extreme hatred of authority, their classmates and what they saw as the status quo. They hatched a plot that started out as nothing more than a fantasy but became a tragic reality when they followed their dreams. Those shitheads are a bleak reminder that terrible outcomes are just as likely to occur when bad, mentally ill or manipulated people follow their dreams. Why should we continue to blanket people everywhere with these simplistic, empty platitudes? Should we always be spreading the message that kids can grow up to be anything they want, when "anything" necessarily includes being bigoted, entitled or greedy?

Regardless of what anyone tells us, don't we all follow our dreams—to a point? After all, everyone follows their dreams until they don't. Every pursuit of every dream has one of the three following outcomes:

1. Success

2. Failure

3. Technical failure (You never stopped trying, but due to some unforeseen circumstance, like death, you are unable to fulfill your dream.)

Failure is always an option. Sometimes it might be good to fail. For example, in mathematics and computer science, there are a number of problems that have no solution. There are countless hours some of the most brilliant minds in history have spent trying to solve problems that, at the time, they didn't realize had no solution. Or sometimes the solution is so complex that they couldn't have possibly solved it with the tools at their disposal. For example, Fermat's last theorem states that there are no three positive integers a, b and c that satisfy $a^n + b^n = c^n$ for any integer n greater than 2. This seemingly simple conjecture was made in 1637, and it took mathematicians 358 years to finally solve it. Fermat famously claimed to have discovered a proof of the theorem, but the margin of the book he wrote it down in was too narrow for it. The final proof was over 150 pages long and utilized modern algebraic geometry and number theory that wasn't discovered until centuries after Fermat's passing. Computer scientists know that there are unsolvable problems, thanks to a formal proof by Alan Turing showing some decision problems are necessarily unsolvable. That a problem has no solution would be good to know before you devote a good chunk of your life going mad trying to solve it. If you accept failure as an option, then you can be free to spend your time in other, more fruitful pursuits, like macramé, bocce or growing exotic fruits.

Technical failure is, for all intents and purposes, the same as regular failure. Not being able to accomplish your goals because you died, ran out of funding, or were put in a predicament that made it impossible for you to continue is basically the universe telling you to give up. Sometimes you should listen. Giving up on your dreams can be a good thing. For example, in 1992 a man named Arthur McElroy attempted to fire a semi-automatic military rifle in a classroom full of students at the University of Nebraska.[25] McElroy was apprehended after his gun jammed, and he served twenty-three years. McElroy didn't make any further attempts after his release, and the world was better for it.

People tell each other to follow their dreams because they are afraid of living lives that are complacent and fraught with regret over settling. Yeah, well, get over it. Almost every decision you make comes with it a cost and a benefit. Our ability to see our dreams come to fruition is a function of how hard we're willing to work, how practical our dreams are and the number of dreams we have. If we have too many, we're diluting ourselves to the point of uselessness. If our dreams are impractical, like winning the lottery, we're setting ourselves up for disappointment. Fuck following your dreams.

FUCK CENSORSHIP

Liberal extremism is equivalent to conservative extremism in one important way: Both lead to censorship. Liberalism wants us all to feel good. Why should anyone ever feel bad about their weight, gender, sexual orientation, race, religion or ethnicity? Any bigoted commentary is frowned upon and outright rejected in most social circles—justly or not. Social media platforms are rife with "terms of service" agreements that abridge the rights of those who join them. Any content deemed offensive for any reason by the platform overlords is to be unceremoniously stricken from the public record.

Conservatives, on the other hand, bristle at liberal censorship, accusing progressives of thought-policing and nannying. Yet the right has its own brand of censorship, in which any criticism of the country is discouraged or outright banned. The "Love It or Leave It" motto is proudly emblazoned on t-shirts and bumper stickers, as if the country is beyond reproach and the one thing you are not allowed to criticize. Your ability to use your "freedom of speech" is called into question when you criticize the very government that allows you to have that freedom of speech. Your ability to express your displeasure with laws and authority ends when you want to burn a flag or criticize our military. Active members of the armed forces often point out in heated debates that you have the freedom to criticize them only because they fight for that freedom—the implication being that you should shut up. And they are correct, insofar as the laws that they are fighting for do protect the speech of those with whom they disagree.

On one hand, most liberals would be pleased if white supremacist or nationalistic hate groups were banished. These groups have extreme beliefs when it comes to race, which may lead to violence against minorities. Similarly, some conservatives aren't shy about their phobia of Islam, citing the exact same justification: Extreme Islamic people act on extremist beliefs to cause violence. While the far end of the liberal spectrum would ban jokes and language that they posit would lead to violence, the far end of the conservative spectrum would ban religious beliefs that they fear would lead to violence. Both conservative and liberal ideologies can lead to censorship, and the feigned outrage both groups level at one another is disingenuous. It's like a race to the bottom to become the most indignant group of whiners.

In 2012 Oklahoma state representative Mike Ritze paid to have a monument of the Ten Commandments—a set of Christian beliefs that has served in part as a guideline for Western law regarding moral and ethical conduct—installed on the state capitol's front lawn.[26] This led to protest from various groups, including the Satanic Temple, which argued that they should have an installation of a Baphomet sculpture, and a Hindu organization requesting a statue of a deity installed alongside the Commandments on the grounds.[27] In 2015, the state's supreme court ruled that the Ten Commandments display was a violation of a provision in the state's constitution that prohibited religious displays on state property.[28] Rather than ceding the argument that all beliefs should have an equal opportunity for representation on state grounds, the state supreme court was forced to defer to the state constitution that prohibits state property from promoting religions. This upset social conservatives who vowed to appeal the ruling, to make an exception in the state constitution for their beliefs.

In 2016 conservative writer Milo Yiannopoulos was banned from Twitter for making jokes at the expense of actor Leslie Jones that were deemed politically incorrect.[29] Yiannopoulos commanded the attention of a large number of conservative followers who took his lead as motivation to harass, imitate and mock Jones. Eventually, Jones left the social media network in protest, citing the overwhelming bullying and harassment as the reason. Her public exodus prompted Twitter administrators to take action and ban Yiannopoulos permanently from their platform. The ban was quick and decisive, yet ambiguous, as Twitter officials wouldn't state which comment or comments specifically caused the ban. Milo's supporters quickly decried the action as censorship, which was hotly debated, as Twitter is a private company. But the most chilling aspect of this silencing is that all record of his alleged infractions has disappeared from the site. There is no opportunity to confront one's accuser, no due process, and no way to appeal. It's an unceremonious silencing at the behest of a company that has decided that your form of expression is no longer valid on their platform. This has led some conservatives to feel targeted on progressive social media platforms like Twitter.[30]

The ugly business of thought-policing extends to both ends of the political spectrum. Whereas the liberal rallying cry has been charges of racism, sexism and homophobia in online social media platforms, a 2015 Harris Poll found that Republicans were nearly twice as likely to be in favor of banning books than their liberal or independent counterparts.[31] Specifically, respondents of the survey who identified as Republican were 14 percent more likely to believe that books on such topics as witchcraft or sorcery should not be available to children in school libraries. The intolerance of ideas didn't end there, however, as Republicans were also more likely to believe that religious texts like the Koran and Torah should not be made available to schoolchildren, and they were 13 percent more likely to believe that books questioning the existence of a divine being "probably" or "definitely" should not be made available in public school libraries.

Everyone is in favor of the idea of free speech, until that speech offends *them*. The people who vocally champion the doctrine of life, liberty and the pursuit of happiness are often the most thin skinned in society. If condoms could be made of their hide, latex manufacturers would face some stiff competition. Fuck censorship.

FUCK BODIES

Virtual reality will make bodies irrelevant. Everything about your shitty body can be fixed in virtual reality, and if you already have a great body, fuck your body anyway. There is life before virtual reality and life after virtual reality. Not that shitty, jittery virtual reality of the early 1990s, with flat-shaded polygons and stupid blocky vistas. There will be a new wave of virtual reality, with full sensory perception, realistic graphics and tactile feedback. It's only a matter of time before virtual reality can interface directly with our brains to trigger any sensory or motor stimulation that we experience. There's nothing that virtual reality can't simulate, short of abstract recursive simulations that theoretical physicists talk about, but nobody cares about that. Go home, nerds.

Virtual reality is better than reality. I can't wait to turn it on, plug in and tune out of life forever. Every single experience I can have in real life can be replicated and enhanced in virtual reality. Why bother with people, bodies and things you don't like? Everything you don't like about yourself can be changed instantly in virtual reality. Want to fix your dumpy ass and busted stomach? No problem. Want a hotter partner? Trivial. Want to eat lunch in Paris? Sure thing, Jacques. Nearly anything is possible in virtual reality, and the experience is not only comparable to real life, but it's also better for so many reasons. For example, going on a vacation to a distant country can be fun and rewarding, but it costs a lot of time and money. It requires taking time off work, and what you can do or see may be limited by language or cultural barriers. In virtual reality, you can have the same experience with none of the drawbacks. Why would anyone care about going anywhere ever again if they can have the same or better experience in virtual reality? And there's nothing stopping you from combining awesome experiences in virtual reality, so enjoy that trip through Luxembourg Gardens in a triceratops-shaped monster truck with machine-gun horns!

One argument that can be made for traveling in real life over virtual reality is that life can afford you the opportunities to meet strangers in a distant land, due to unforeseen circumstances. For example, the people you might meet unexpectedly when you take shelter from the rain in a small café, or a local shop owner who might give you memorable service. Or you might meet a nice couple who run a family-owned bed-and-breakfast. Or maybe you'll meet some other excited travelers in a hostel, who trade travel tips with you. All of those experiences can be had in virtual reality, only better. The nice couple running a bed-and-breakfast can be nicer, swinging and down to bang. The beds can be bigger, the food more varied, and instead of rain, you can be taking shelter from lava, soup or an alien invasion. By comparison, life is boring.

All of those seemingly "random" events that happen in real life can occur virtually as well. Or, conversely, you can choose to limit random events, so that you can take a vacation without chance events that may hamper experiences you would have in real life, like blackout dates at theme parks, street closures, labor strikes, or running out of the mahimahi. Hours of operation for stores and museums would be irrelevant. In fact, time and daylight as we experience them would be irrelevant. It can be any time of day you want, any time you want.

We are three technological milestones away from complete virtual reality immersion. The first of these is to simulate tactile feedback, temperature, altitude and natural climate experiences, such as wind. This technology already exists with haptic gloves, fans, heating and cooling elements and hydraulic platforms to simulate ascension and gravity. There's even some experimentation with 360-degree treadmills that allow people to run and walk in place. It's only a matter of time before some visionary Armenian author inspires an enterprising engineer to put all of these elements together and implement this full-body immersion. The second milestone is to simulate scents, which would require real-time synthesis of chemicals to create synthetic smells that would be released in specific environments, triggered by events you experience in the virtual world. For example, entering a bakery would emit fragrances of fresh pies or burnt bread, if the bakery happens to be run by virtual idiots. The third and final step will be complete neural connectivity, so that every sensory experience—including taste, hunger, thirst and perspiration—can be directly triggered programmatically from within the virtual-reality application. This final step would completely take over our senses, making the previous two milestones not only irrelevant but also our entire bodies obsolete. It would be tantamount to plugging headphone jacks into your computer, except for every sense that we have, not just hearing. It would create a virtual world so believable that it may be indistinguishable from real life. All our energy needs can be met with food drips that provide all the nutrients we require, while our flavor sensors are triggered to experience anything we could possibly want to taste.

All of this is good, and I can't wait for it. Though there's one important caveat we may need to address: learning experiences. Real life doesn't have a good track record. It's often too hot, too cold, too boring and full of annoying people and experiences that we can't control. Virtual reality is a comfortable reprieve from real life, and if we can tailor our experiences in virtual reality like we do with news and opinions online, would we ever choose to experience things that make us sad, annoyed, frustrated, or angry? What about sensory experiences we'd rather avoid, such as jitters, anxiety, or embarrassment? Some of these seemingly frustrating experiences in life can be valuable opportunities to learn and grow. Virtual reality may increase our knowledge but limit our wisdom. Knowledge is knowing how to speak, but wisdom is knowing when to speak. If we can simply avoid awkward situations, such as saying something inappropriate at a dinner party or committing unintentional cultural taboos like asking an American how much money they make, how will we ever learn the valuable lessons of tempering our dialogue and learning to deal with embarrassment? And what about the ethical concerns of manufacturers abusing the thirst sensation to sell you virtual beverages that would quench your thirst every time they opt to advertise their products? If the sensation of having your thirst or hunger sated is an arbitrary programmatic trigger, is it ethical for a company to force you to experience discomfort until you pay them to make it stop?

Still, being a dumb fucking idiot who knows a lot of facts, lacks wisdom and may be held hostage to corporate whims may be a small price to pay for being able to live in a world where you can ride the back of a flying dragon while you wail on a machine-gun guitar and tower-buzz hot peasants in bikinis. Sign me up forever.

FUCK THE APPROVAL
OF YOUR LOVED ONES

Disappointing your loved ones is a huge relief. It's the exact moment you're liberated from the expectations of others, and you're absolved from fulfilling the hopes that someone else had imposed on your life. The failure to meet these expectations and dreams makes you a badass. You become impenetrable to nagging, impervious to guilt and indifferent to deadlines. You can't fall if you're facedown on the ground. Once you've tripped, you can't trip any further.

Take, for example, the disappointment your parents might feel at your choice of a major that doesn't meet their expectations. First of all, who cares? Their disappointment doesn't cost you anything. They don't approve of what you want to study in school? Good, fuck 'em! Why should their opinion on your intellectual pursuits matter? Do you also let them pick your movies and books? How long did they think they could micromanage your life? Eighteen years? Twenty? You're a sentient being, and earning your parents' disappointment after a large academic decision should provide a reprieve from their overbearing wishes for you—even if their wishes are prudent and wise. Part of being an adult is having the ability to decide what mistakes you want to make in life. Disappointing your parents early and often will condition them into giving up on you. That will free you from the knee-jerk decisions you may be making out of spite or rebellion.

Sometimes we end up dating people who are terrible for us, simply to spite our parents. A classic example is a girl who might date a man with a "bad boy" image, in part because her parents are overbearing, and this minor transgression is an attempt at becoming independent. Similarly, people sometimes go out of their way to date outside of their race or ethnicity, if they sense that their parents would disapprove of such a union. There are few things more satisfying than disappointing prejudiced people, and it's especially sweet when those people are your parents. Rather than worrying about running afoul of their elaborate blueprints for your life, why not disappoint them early and be done with it? It's our choice as adults to bring another life into this world, and then we arrogantly decide what's best for them while simultaneously espousing the disingenuous belief that they have free agency. We tell our children they can grow up to be anything they want, but if they fall short of our expectations, we punish them with our disappointment and guilt without stopping to ask ourselves: Is this fair?

The hopes that our loved ones impose on us are often a form of manipulation, especially when you're beholden to them for financial aid. I've witnessed friends spend years in school studying subjects they had no passion for, date people they weren't in love with, take religious pilgrimages they weren't interested in and even have children they didn't want, all for the sake of not disappointing their relatives. Almost always, they justify their bad decisions as some kind of age-old wisdom received from their parents' generation. The subjects they studied without passion will be lucrative, the religious pilgrimages will be seen as enlightening (though at the expense of other personal enlightenment they could have achieved) and the children will be seen as a blessing that they couldn't have appreciated had they not been browbeaten into procreation.

Yet with all the decisions we let other people make in our lives, we have lingering in the backs of our minds a small but unavoidable kernel of self-doubt. It's the creeping suspicion that you may have not made the right choice or, at the very least, the best choice for you. There's a possibility that you could have done better had they not meddled. It's the lingering notion that the received wisdom of past generations wasn't even wisdom to begin with. After all, why do we take for granted that familial tradition passed on from generation to generation is actual wisdom? Just because your parents did it, and their parents did it before them, doesn't mean it was good in the first place. Racist parents who pass on their fears and prejudices to their progeny, or parents committed to the cultural tradition of female genital mutilation for no reason other than rote tradition, are just a few of many examples.

There is no virtue in pleasing others just for the sake of pleasing them. Professionally, this disposition is seen as belonging to the cowardly "yes-man"—someone who will always agree with you and will kowtow to your every whim. It's not a quality that commands respect. Breaking free from familial expectations is the training ground for breaking free from society's will. People who can't stand up to their parents, employers or colleagues when bad decisions are made aren't equipped with the faculties of leadership. They're not prepared for the challenges of life, let alone parenthood.

Take, for example, meeting a deadline for a work assignment. If you don't meet that deadline, your employer is let down and a little upset, but it's a small price to pay for being able to get back to work without that impending deadline exhausting your precious time and mental resources. Worrying about things is mentally taxing. Disappointing someone is like finally setting down a huge sack of groceries or peeing after you've been holding it in all day. It lets you refocus your efforts and actually accomplish what you set out to do without the baggage of guilt. The moment you realize that you've fallen short of someone's expectations and affirmed their fears, you're absolved of the lingering specter of their hopes.

Disappointment is freedom.

FUCK OLD IDEAS

The belief that there are no new ideas is the lazy thinker's mantra. To come up with new ideas is trivial. In fact, it's harder to come up with an unoriginal idea than an original one. The reason some people think that there are no new ideas is that they're trying to solve the same small set of problems, like how to fit into a mason jar the ingredients for yet another shitty dessert nobody will like. When you expand your scope of problems, you start to force yourself to think creatively. For example, determining when a self-driving car should drive off a cliff to avoid plowing into a group of pedestrians is a problem worth thinking about.

People are lazy and lack breadth of vision, so as soon as they find a satisfactory solution to a problem, they stop trying. That's the definition of a C grade in school: satisfactory. It takes mental work and ingenuity to come up with a new solution to an old problem. But old problems are the idiot's crutch. It's almost as trivial to find a new problem as it is to find the solution to that problem. For example, finding a way to balance the benefits of technology that always "listens" to you for prompts with the goal of retaining your privacy. It's a problem that may take some forethought, trial and error, and analysis. Yet it's a problem that isn't discussed nearly as often as, say, the best way to hang a roll of toilet paper. The lazy thinker occupies him- or herself with small, trivial problems that everyone has considered ad nauseam. It's not that there are no new ideas, it's that people are dipshits.

Coming up with a new or novel idea may be as simple as coming up with a sentence that's never been written. After all, if you can't write it down, it probably isn't an idea.* There are 10^{570} possible sentence combinations in the English language.[32] Being that there have only been an estimated 130 million books written, encompassing the entirety of mankind's published history,[33] and assuming the average book has roughly 65,000 words (250 words per page x 260 pages per book) and that the average sentence has 20 words in it,[34] that's 3,250 sentences per book x 130 million books = 422.5 billion sentences ever published by humanity. Let's go ahead and round that up to 500 billion. Hell, go ahead and quadruple it if you want to count newspapers, magazines, satirical websites, letters, diaries, emails, interoffice memos and grocery lists. So if you try to string together a sequence of words that have never been written before, your odds of repeating a sentence is roughly $2 / 10^{558}$, or a 0 percent likelihood. And that's just going by the total number of sentences, assuming each sentence is a unique thought (it isn't). Many sentences are nonsensical, mundane or only serve as exposition for a story or a reference in scientific literature. Original thoughts are rare, yet trivial to produce.

The people who criticize ideas as being derivative can barely hide their seething jealousy of those who possess true ingenuity. It's the intellectual equivalent of an unaccomplished loser criticizing a popular band for being "talentless." Yet these critics can't

---

* Art falls into this category because art can be reduced to pictographs, and pictography is the basis of many Asian languages, so shut your stupid mouth before you even start with that shit.

replicate the success of these so-called untalented bands, as if the reason were because they don't deign to. The truth of the situation, which they aren't wise enough to suss out, is that the truly brilliant often make what they do seem easy. This book is one such case. For example, there are plenty of shit jokes and cuss words in this book, which serve to disarm the reader, making him or her more suggestible to the ideas I present. By the time the reader realizes it, it's too late, because the ideas are already absorbed. The sentence you just read was an original idea, about an original book and a novel approach to presenting ideas, demonstrating that new ideas do exist. You just read the literal construction of a new idea to prove that new ideas are easy to come up with. Boom.

FUCK RAISING AWARENESS

Raising awareness is like tweeting about a fire in your kitchen. Social network chatter, bumper stickers and blog posts do nothing to solve any problem. It's the laziest form of activism in existence. People who do it are hoping that someone—anyone—else will do something about it, instead of them.

There's a well-known psychological phenomenon called the "bystander effect," where individuals won't offer to help people in need if other people are present. The effect was first demonstrated by social psychologists John Darley and Bibb Latané in 1968 to help explain why dozens of bystanders allegedly witnessed the murder of a New York woman without intervening. They conducted experiments and found that one of the reasons people don't intervene is "diffusion of responsibility,"[35] or the assumption that one of the other bystanders has already called for help or will take action. Many people hold the mistaken belief that the more people who are aware of a problem, the more likely it is that someone else will take action to help. And that's exactly why raising awareness is not only lazy, do-nothing slacktivism, but it may be doing more harm than good.

Although some of the awareness campaigns that people promote are for problems much larger than any individual can tackle, there are things individuals can do to help, such as donate money or volunteer their time or services. And therein lies the problem with awareness campaigns: There's rarely a call to action. It's all awareness, no activity.

Asking people to change their profile pictures or to use a hashtag campaign on social networks is feel-good fluff and false charity. People participate because it costs them nothing, and they get the feeling of having accomplished something. When our lives are largely filled with the minutia of checking email, text messages and clearing notifications from apps that pester us ad nauseam, we feel unproductive for wasting so much time doing effectively jack shit. All of the things we should have been doing instead, like taking care of our bills, hygiene, homework, interpersonal relationships with friends and family, activism and charity, fall by the wayside. Then guilt starts seeping into our lives.

When we see an opportunity to check one of those items— activism or charity—off our list, without so much as lifting our fingers from our keyboards, we click away like happy idiots. The most insidious kind of gratification is that which is felt for something we didn't actually accomplish. It ends progress and personal growth. It makes us lazier, duller and more complacent. Why keep running if you think you've crossed the finish line?

It's rare for any of these campaigns to accomplish anything, but it's not impossible. In July of 2014, a viral awareness campaign called the "ALS Ice Bucket Challenge" started spreading around on the Internet. The aim was to raise money for amyotrophic lateral sclerosis, or Lou Gehrig's disease. Unlike other slacker awareness campaigns for slacker idiots, this one had a call to action associated with it: People were encouraged to either donate to the ALS charity or dump a bucket of ice water over their heads. While many people took it as an opportunity to show off and garner attention from their easily amused friends and family members, many people did actually donate. In fact, some people did both. The campaign was a phenomenal success, raising over $100 million in thirty days.[36] In fact, the campaign was so successful that it was criticized for taking focus away from other more pressing causes, like chronic obstructive pulmonary disease, which results in eighteen times more fatalities but received only $7 million in donations that year.[37]

Another rare instance where raising awareness may have helped accomplish a goal was the push for gay marriage equality in the United States. The U.S. Supreme Court was considering arguments in favor of legalizing gay marriage, so in 2013, an advocacy group called Human Rights Campaign encouraged people to change their profile pictures to red and pink equality signs to show solidarity with marginalized lesbian, gay, bisexual and transgendered people.[38] The campaign took the Internet by storm and demonstrated the shifting tides of public opinion, which may have served to persuade some people still on the fence about the issue. If it seems popular to support a position, or, conversely, unpopular not to support it, it may persuade people to be sympathetic to your cause. It's one of the few times in life that suggestible people are useful for anything more than just kindling for a bonfire.

The reason the pink equality campaign worked is that the goal was to change public perception. Historically, one of the best ways to influence the public has been through traditional advertising in print, billboards, television and radio. When people changed their profile pictures to a pink equal sign in support of gay equality, it was in essence a high-powered advertising campaign, but for the low cost of zero dollars. It worked because the means of achieving the end result was as effective as a traditional advertising campaign.

Unfortunately, these cases of productive slacktivism are the exceptions, not the rule. In 2013 the Swedish organization UNI-

CEF decided to launch a new advertising campaign to combat apathetic charity, aptly titled "Likes don't save lives."[39] Yes, the Internet just got called out by the United Nations children's fund. When a humanitarian organization that exists to help children and mothers in developing countries thinks you're full of shit, it might be time to reflect on your life choices.

The UNICEF campaign included a series of YouTube videos with a couple going to various establishments trying to pay for goods with "likes" to demonstrate that clicks don't translate to cash (Fig. 19). One of the most poignant of these ads showcased a ten-year-old boy who said he was worried that he might become sick like his mother, because then nobody would be around to look after his brother, but that everything will "be all right" because UNICEF Sweden had 177,000 "likes" on Facebook. The video ends with the slogan "Likes don't save lives. Money does."[40]

Like us on Facebook, and we will vaccinate zero children against polio.

We have nothing against likes, but vaccine costs money. Please buy polio vaccine at unicef.se. It will only cost you 4 €, but will save the lives of 12 children.

unicef

Fig. 19: The currency of "likes" has cured approximately zero people to date.

Another, more egregious instance of slacktivism seems to have permeated the campaign of the U.S. charity Invisible Children in 2012, which drew attention to the criminal leader of the Ugandan guerrilla movement, the Lord's Resistance Army (LRA). Founded in 2004, in 2012 its campaign centered around a thiry-minute documentary, which received over 100 million views in its first six days alone, and was spread on social networks using the #Kony2012 hashtag. Its primary call to action? To get people to buy a thirty dollar "action kit," which included a t-shirt, pins, stickers and a poster—because when I think of taking action against a rogue military regime, I rush to get my stickers. The goal of the kit seemed to be to raise awareness of Joseph Kony on the international stage and not much else, supposedly to encourage governments to bring Kony to justice. In what may have been the largest experiment on the bystander effect to date, over $31.9 million in unrestricted funds was raised by the group in 2012[41] apparently to encourage someone else to solve the problem by raising awareness. Raising awareness requires t-shirts, stickers and a robust Twitter account. The charity even states as much on their mission statement, which claims its goal is to "raise awareness and [educate] the U.S. about the atrocities, exploitations and abuse of invisible children throughout the world."[42] One could argue that there are usually better uses for contributions than raising awareness of a problem, like tackling contemporary issues that might be plaguing Ugandans. By 2012 international governments—the parties that could take action against an armed force—were already well aware of the LRA's atrocities, which undermined the presumed necessity or even usefulness of the awareness they were raising. What's needed to bring Kony to justice isn't his face on a yoga mom's t-shirt. Instead, you'd want to enlist local and international authorities, soldiers, weapons, ammunition, armored transport and one extra bullet with his name on it.

The LRA has been classified as a terrorist organization by the U.S. State Department since 2001,[43] and the International Criminal Court issued arrest warrants for Kony and other top LRA commanders in 2005,[44] a full seven years before the Kony 2012 campaign. In 2008, the United States was involved in an offensive against the LRA, code-named "Operation Lightning Thunder," four years before Kony 2012.[45] And in 2010, the Lord's Resistance Army Disarmament and Northern Uganda Recovery Act of 2009 was signed by President Barack Obama,[46] which specifically acknowledged and enumerated the LRA's atrocities. And even five months before the release of the viral Kony video, President Obama authorized the use of a hundred or so Special Forces troops in Uganda to assist in the removal of the militia's leadership.[47] So what, exactly, did we get for all this awareness, millions of dollars and some noisy banging of pots and pans? Not much, since the campaign didn't bring Joseph Kony to justice, and his name has largely faded from people's minds.

One possible positive outcome of the movement was that in 2013, the United States offered a $5 million bounty for the capture of Kony,[48] but it's hard to say what role the campaign played—if any—in setting this bounty. Even if we're to attribute 100 percent of the reason this bounty exists to Kony 2012, it seems like a paltry sum compared to the charity's take of $31 million—roughly six times more. If bounties do motivate people to help capture fugitives, and they often do, the implication is that the Kony campaign could have been more effective if it had simply offered the entire sum as a reward for his capture. Or many millions could have been used as reparations paid directly to victims, or to build infrastructure in a country where the average monthly household income is $88 USD.[49] Or for reconstructive surgery for victims of the LRA abuse, many of whom have suffered mutilation of their lips, ears, noses and fingers. And a lot less on YouTube videos, in a country where less than 15 percent of the population has Internet access[50] and fewer than nine computers exist for every thousand people. The video was targeting Americans and U.S. politicians, which came across as incredibly tone deaf and condescending to some Ugandans, who weren't shy about sharing their opinions.

During a screening in Uganda shortly after its release, the documentary was met with anger, confusion and skirmishes.[51] The screening ended prematurely when police fired live rounds into the air, the crowd pelted organizers with stones and tear gas was fired into the crowd.[52] One woman expressed anger at the commercial nature of popularizing Kony with merchandise, likening it to selling Osama Bin Laden trinkets after 9/11 to raise awareness for his capture.[53] If that idea sounds offensive and condescending to Americans, that's because it is. People didn't need Osama Bin Laden bracelets and t-shirts to know who he was. Osama Bin Laden is a good case study, because as far as exposure and fame goes, he had about as much as a human could possibly get. It took the United States over a decade to find Bin Laden, and that's with a $25 million bounty and a maximum level of "awareness," as almost every major newspaper in the world covered him at one point in time. Even if Kony had the same level of exposure, there's no guarantee that he'd be brought to justice in a timely manner— or ever.

Lack of awareness isn't the reason criminals like Kony remain at large. His status as a fugitive isn't contingent upon his ability to blend into Seattle coffee shops unnoticed. Kony has evaded capture for a complex set of reasons unrelated to "awareness," not least of which are failed negotiations, broken truces, the difficult nature of tracking guerrilla armies in dense jungles, lack of actionable intelligence and the fact that his group had been driven out of Uganda years before the documentary's release.[54,55]

The folly of slacktivist campaigns like these is that they fail to take the next step, from awareness to action. Hanging posters in coffee shops about a Ugandan general—who was already being hunted by South African authorities for years—won't help bring him to justice. Also, it may do more harm than good by giving the impression that someone is doing something about the problem, even when they aren't. Fuck raising awareness.

FUCK BEING COLD

Being cold is for suckers. I'm never cold, because I'm not an idiot. Any time I feel cold, which is never, I realize I can control the situation by moving out of the way of the thing that's making me cold, like a vent or an open window. You can always control how cold you are just by moving. If you find yourself in an environment where you can't control the temperature or your proximity to the thing that's making you cold, then you're one of the aforementioned idiots and/or suckers I'm referring to, and you might be more interested in complaining than solving the problem.

Not being cold is the easiest thing to do in life. Even birds have figured out how to not be cold: They go someplace warmer. Cats grow out their fur in the winter—unless they are hairless cats, which feel like they are made entirely of penis skin, so who cares? Dogs whine until they manipulate and guilt their owners into letting them inside. Snakes freeze to death because nobody cares, not even them. Basically, everything and everyone worthwhile on Earth finds a way to stay warm. Why can't you?

Every single person who has a home has multiple sets of clothes to wear. It's like a precondition for existence, unless you *just* escaped from a mental hospital and are being chased by bloodhounds. Yet few think to stop complaining and put on some of the extra clothes they own. Complaining about being cold when you have more clothes to wear is like complaining about being hungry when there's food in your mouth. Just swallow it; it's right there.

Spicy food is a great way to stay warm; it's like a heater for your throat. There's no excuse to complain that any point along your digestive tract is cold if you possess anything spicy. Every time I see kids crying because they're cold, I always give them some ghost pepper hot sauce. The parents usually rush their kids away from me because I've done such a good job. Kids who eat hot sauce grow back hair, and back hair keeps you warm. That's why I'm never cold: I have back hair all over my body, even my scalp. Fuck being cold.

FUCK FEIGNED SYMPATHY

Conniving mothers who try to guilt their children into eating dinner use the classic platitude that "Starving children in China would be grateful for that meal." First of all, your mother can't rule out the possibility that maybe her food actually does taste shitty, and that starving kids in China would agree. Second, when you have to invoke starving people as the ones who could credibly appreciate the meal you've prepared, you fortify the original objections to your food.

But that's beside the point. Do you really care about starving children in China? If so, why are they only invoked when coercing someone into eating something you prepared? Shouldn't we care about starving people all the time? After all, if we know people are suffering and don't do anything about it, aren't we morally bankrupt? And isn't it made worse when we use someone's suffering as a rhetorical device to guilt someone into eating food that resulted from a perfect vacuum of expertise and talent?

People barely care about the homeless in their own neighborhoods, so why would you expect anyone to believe that you care about people you've never seen, met, or even know for a fact exist in China, Africa or Detroit?

People love stories that make them feel more compassionate than they are. We love the narratives we tell ourselves every time we go to the grocery store and see a package of cage-free, pasture-fed, no-hormone, locally grown, sustainable, organic chicken eggs. There's an entire paragraph of narrative to consider every time you just want to make a fucking omelet.

If people cared about the plight of those suffering, they'd do more to help them. We don't, so just like we should stop lying to ourselves about the narratives with which we select our foods, it's time to stop lying to ourselves about how good and compassionate we think we are. All people have their limits of compassion and tolerance for suffering. When we hit our threshold, we tune it out. For some of us, that tolerance is zero. If you think back on the last seven days of your life and consider the number of times you've thought about someone who was homeless or suffering, and that number is close to zero, congratulations: You're one of these people. You're more concerned with the appearance of propriety than caring, and using the plight of famine to guilt others into eating your culinary abortion is doubly shameful.

FUCK PEOPLE WHO
WANT TO GET RID OF JERKS

One of the most dangerous colloquial phrases is "Don't be a jerk." Most people read this statement on a message board or inspirational quote somewhere and accept it as a truism, without expending a single joule of energy considering why.

Being a jerk is bad, right? And all things bad are by definition not good. So if it's not good, we should avoid it—that's the prevailing theory parroted by well-intentioned hipsters, anyway. The problem with this thinking is that it fails to consider one important fucking fact:

Jerks get shit done.

Ever wanted someone to shut up in a theater but didn't want to rock the boat yourself? There's always a jerk out there willing to put his hand in the flame for you. You know that asshole in your break room who drops ideological turds about how homosexuals are evil or subtly racist remarks to see if anyone's on board with him? He's a jerk, yes, but it's another jerk that's going to stand up to that guy. Sometimes the solution to a jerk is another jerk.

Complaining about your food or bill in a restaurant will likely result in one or more of the wait staff getting reprimanded, or a manager having a bad day, which makes you a jerk, especially when the alternative is only some minor inconvenience. But if your grievances are just and the restaurant never goes on to correct their mistakes, many more people will experience their shitty service and suffer because of it, all because you decided to be meek instead of cocksure.

Mercifully, jerks are the first ones to eat at parties. It's far too often the case that most partygoers will be too shy or timid to be the first to serve themselves. Jerks don't care, and they'll jump on the grenade of impropriety, setting a precedent that liberates all other partygoers to follow suit. Nobody wants to be first at a buffet line in a wedding because they'll appear immodest or eager, which holds up the food line for everyone including the bride and groom, who are in all likelihood famished and over everyone's bullshit. A jerk's indifference is your bounty.

A study published in the *Journal of Personality and Social Psychology* in 2012 found that overconfident individuals—a.k.a. jerks—were not only perceived as having higher status by others, but they were also perceived as being more competent than individuals with more accurate self-perceptions.[56] Due to their indefensible higher status, these overly confident assholes often end up in positions of management and authority, which explains why so many people think their bosses are incompetent. It's not just your imagination—your boss is most likely incompetent—yet you are their subordinate precisely because they are better at commanding the respect of others for no reason other than that they are full of themselves. Ironically, this provides jerks with psychological benefits such as higher self-esteem, which in turn leads to better mental health and can make them more motivated, which positively correlates to higher salaries and positions, making them even more confident in their abilities and giving them even higher status, until they become president of the United States. The president is often the least competent person in the world, if global criticism is any indication.

It's commonly considered bad driving etiquette to perform a late merge from a lane that's ending into one with traffic. The Colorado Department of Transportation found that this behavior not only increased the flow of traffic by 15 percent but also that the length of a merge line decreased by 50 percent when drivers observed these "rude" driving behaviors.[57] So the department began promoting the late merge with road signs in 2006, suggesting that drivers "use both lanes to the merge point." In other words, they were imploring drivers to be jerks and the world was better off for it.

General George S. Patton, the famous general who commanded the U.S. Third Army in World War II, was by all accounts an asshole. He was famously reprimanded for slapping two U.S. Army soldiers who were suffering from shell shock, a condition that later came to be known as post-traumatic stress disorder—a disorder that Patton didn't believe existed. He even went so far as to threaten one of the soldiers with a pistol:

> *You're going back to the front lines and you may get shot and killed, but you're going to fight. If you don't, I'll stand you up against a wall and have a firing squad kill you on purpose. In fact, I ought to shoot you myself . . . It makes my blood boil to think of a yellow bastard being babied. I won't have those cowardly bastards hanging around our hospitals. We'll probably have to shoot them some time anyway, or we'll raise a breed of morons.*[58]

Yet in spite of his brash commanding approach, Patton went on to give some of the most inspiring speeches to his troops, including his famous speech given before D-Day on June 5, 1944, in which he suggested lubricating tank treads with the bodies of Nazis:

All through your army career you men have bitched about what you call "this chicken-shit drilling." That is all for a purpose—to ensure instant obedience to orders and to create constant alertness. This must be bred into every soldier. I don't give a fuck for a man who is not always on his toes. But the drilling has made veterans of all you men. You are ready! A man has to be alert all the time if he expects to keep on breathing. If not, some German son-of-a-bitch will sneak up behind him and beat him to death with a sock full of shit . . .

We'll win this war, but we'll win it only by fighting and showing the Germans that we've got more guts than they have or ever will have. We're not just going to shoot the bastards, we're going to rip out their living goddamned guts and use them to grease the treads of our tanks. We're going to murder those lousy Hun cocksuckers by the bushel-fucking-basket.

Patton went on to lead the U.S. Army in some of the most successful military campaigns across Europe, advancing into Nazi Germany and providing crucial support to beleaguered Allied forces. His contributions to the war effort were incalculable—and no one would dispute that he was the very definition of a jerk.

FUCK VEGETARIANS WHO
WON'T EAT LEFTOVER MEAT

The idea behind vegetarianism and veganism is to turn a boy-cott into a lifestyle. The product and industry they're boycotting? Meat. The idea is that by abstaining from food that tastes good and provides essential nutrients not found in plants, there will be less demand for it. Less demand will result in less production, which will result in fewer animals being killed. Then everyone can play grab-ass in the forest while eating twigs and living stupidly ever after.

The boycott rationale, while doing nothing to address the unjust discrimination of vegetarians choosing to protect animal life forms over plant life forms, is at least based on a logical foun-dation. Where that foundation starts to break apart is when you realize that most vegetarians will even abstain from eating leftover meat. If someone orders a meat dish at a restaurant and can't fin-ish his or her food, the rationale of boycotting animal products to reduce demand is irrelevant. The vegetarian's boycott can't un-kill the animal, and it can't reduce demand, since the animal has already been ordered.

In fact, not eating leftover meat means that an animal's sacri-fice will have gone in vain. Vegetarians should not only have the obligation to eat leftover meat out of reverence for the animal, but they should prioritize eating these leftovers over any other food. There's nothing precluding a vegetarian from being a self-righteous idiot the rest of his life, but for the purposes of his boycott, not eating animals that are already dead through no fault of his own won't make a lick of difference in the demand for meat.

There's no surer sign of a vegetarian being an asshole than when he or she abstains from a turkey dinner. Turkeys are usually large enough to feed six to ten people, and there are almost always leftovers. The argument could be made that the leftovers could still be consumed by nonvegetarians in later meals, which would reduce the number of new meat dishes an omnivore would procure, thus still having a net reduction in animal product demand. The problem with this theory is that it's bullshit. Specifically because of the following reasons:

1. It assumes that the omnivore will definitely eat the leftovers if the vegetarian doesn't. Sometimes omnivores get tired of eating the same meal for multiple days in a row, or they might eat a meal that contains no meat at all, like a salad, causing the leftover meat to go to waste.

2. It assumes that there will always be enough leftovers to replace an entire meal. Sometimes the amount of food left over is only a few morsels.

3. It overestimates the impact that replacing a few servings will have on the meat industry.

If a vegetarian abstained from eating leftover meat, and those leftovers were enough to constitute an entire meal, and that meal would have necessarily been consumed by the omnivore, and the omnivore definitely would have eaten meat for the meal those leftovers were replacing, then—and only then—would the argument hold any water. But that is a complex set of conditions that would occur rarely, if ever. The U.S. meat industry produces 47.3 billion pounds (21.5 billion kg) of commercial red meat[59] and about 36 billion pounds (16.3 billion kg) of chicken.[60] The market regularly tolerates fluctuations of at least 4 percent year to year, as meat production was down by 4 percent in May of 2015[61] but up 5 percent in June compared to the same month the year before.[62] Being that 3.2 percent of American adults are vegetarian,[63] their entire lifestyle as a group has less impact than the whimsical fluctuations in demand by omnivores. The subset impact of abstaining from eating leftover meat that meets all three conditions above approaches zero.

Even worse are the staunch vegetarians who refuse to eat food that accidentally touched a piece of meat. These ideological blowhards aren't changing anything by abstaining from this food. They're just being dogmatic assholes for the sake of vanity. When abstaining makes no appreciable difference to the meat industry's bottom line, boycotting it has more to do with a person's psychology than making a tangible difference in the world. Want to make a real difference? Become an omnivore.

A study published in 2012 in the journal *Elementa: Science of the Anthropocene* found that when analyzing diet scenarios that would maximize land-carrying capacity—the number of people being fed per unit of land area—that a blend of an omnivore diet with a heavier emphasis on vegetables was better than a purely vegan diet because grazing utilizes nonarable land unsuitable for crops.[64] Omnivores? More like awesomnivores.

FUCK YOUR ARBITRARY
SYMPATHY COMPLEX

The sympathy vegetarians and vegans show toward animals, as opposed to plants, insects and bacteria, is arbitrary speciesism. The key to freeing them from this arbitrary sympathy may lie in the creation of a robot created solely for the purpose of abuse.

Hear me out.

Over 75 percent of vegetarians and vegans surveyed abstain from meat for ethical reasons,[65] as opposed to religious, flavor, economic, or allergic reasons. They don't eat meat because they feel empathy for the pain animals may feel in captivity or while being slaughtered. This empathy is rooted in anthropomorphism—the projection of human emotions, experiences and qualities onto animals and inanimate objects. Vegetarians reason that animals exhibit signs of intelligence and pain, similar to the way humans do, so inflicting pain upon them is morally wrong. The father of the modern animal rights movement, Peter Singer, wrote the landmark book that established many of the arguments and tenets of this movement, *Animal Liberation: The Definitive Classic of the Animal Movement.*

In his book, Singer argues that "we ought to consider the interests of animals because they have interests" and that by excluding them from "the sphere of moral concern," that humans treat animals as if their interests do not warrant consideration outside of the benefits humans derive from them.[66] Yeah, no shit? Singer's assumption that animals have interests requires us to project some degree of human ambition and purpose onto animals. Singer completely sidesteps the fact that plants do show surprisingly similar metabolic responses to pain; for example, researcher Dianna Bowles found that when she wounded a tomato leaf, she could measure an electrical response in an unwounded leaf in a different area on the same plant.[67] She eliminated the possibility that these signals were transmitted chemically by icing the plant's stem to block chemical transmission from the wounded leaf through the stem. This mechanism parallels the way in which neurons transmit electrical signals in the human central nervous system. For the concept of pain to be such a central component of the argument for the animal rights cause, activists like Singer ignore the possibility that plants experience a type of pain we still don't fully understand.

If we are to argue, as many vegetarians believe, that inflicting pain is bad, and that plants feel pain, then we would have to either starve (painfully) to death or else concede that some suffering is necessary for life. Rather than tackle this tricky proposition in his book, Singer simply avoids it with a supersized portion of confirmation bias, by suggesting that "there is no reliable evidence that plants are capable of feeling pleasure or pain," and that "nothing resembling a central nervous system has been found in plants." That's a heavy-handed, inaccurate conclusion, as there are many parallels between the ways in which plants and humans feel. In his book *What a Plant Knows*, author Daniel Chamovitz acknowledges that plants feel mechanical stimulation, although he doesn't consider this "pain" in the sense that the plants aren't able to move away from it.[68]

Singer seems to agree when he says, "It is difficult to imagine why species that are incapable of moving away from a source of pain or using the perception of pain to avoid death in any other way should have evolved the capacity to feel pain." The difficulty someone might have in "imagining" (concocting) a reason for why a species might evolve the capacity to feel pain is irrelevant to whether or not a species has evolved the ability to feel pain. Researchers have shown that a type of plant known as *Mimosa pudica*, or "shy plant," will close its leaves when touched and that this phenomenon stops temporarily when researchers administer anesthetics to the plant.[69] There's even research showing that plants use the perception of "pain" to avoid death, by emitting gaseous signals from damaged plant tissues to alert predators of the herbivore that damaged it, which is tantamount to calling in the cavalry when under attack. These gases can be surprisingly targeted, varying by time of day and the type of herbivore attacking the plant.[70]

The only reason vegetarians can justify their diets is because of the arrogant assumption that, because plant and bacterial life don't exhibit emotions and can't express themselves like animals, it must be morally acceptable to slaughter these life forms. These "ethical" animal rights activists are exhibiting a prime example of the inability-to-disconfirm cognitive bias, or the rejection of any evidence that contradicts their beliefs. If plants had faces and expressed pain or sadness when they were killed, I would contend that vegetarians would either have to reconsider the immorality of eating animals or else starve to death. Hopefully, the latter.

It's in that spirit I propose the creation of an AbuseBot: a robot created solely for abuse. The AbuseBot would be a toy robot that is intentionally anthropomorphized with a face that clearly exhibits emotions. Of course, any emotions it exhibits are purely programmatic, as the robot would be nonfeeling and nonsentient like any other toy. Any emotions it displayed would depend on the instructions it was programmed to show in response to certain stimulus. For example, a hit or a slap with a certain force would trigger a preprogrammed "sad" emotion. The robot could be programmed with a complex set of emotional responses to abuse, from frowning to crying, even cowering in fear when audio sensors detect that someone has entered the room.

Any reasonable person who abused this robot would know that the emotions it was exhibiting were not real. It has no central nervous system. Everything AbuseBot does is an algorithmic response that someone programmed it to have. Yet I would posit that vegetarians and vegans would feel discomfort abusing this robot, even though no actual abuse will have transpired. Nonsentient beings can't be abused, since they have no capacity to think or feel.

Any vegetarian who had a moral objection to abusing AbuseBot would then have to concede that their objection is irrational. I also suspect that if multiple AbuseBots with varying degrees of response to abuse, from low to high, were tested, there would be a proportional response from vegans and vegetarians. The more dismay an AbuseBot exhibits, the more distraught the abuser would feel. This experiment would serve to demonstrate that a vegetarian's ethical concerns aren't rooted in preventing actual suffering so much as anthropomorphic projection of human feelings and emotions onto nonhuman beings—animals and, in this case, inanimate objects.

Vegetarians and vegans might accuse me of speciesism. I'm completely fine with that. But aren't they guilty of kingdomism? Why would it be morally superior to arbitrarily choose animal life as more worthy of sympathy than vegetable, bacterial or fungal life forms? What's more, even a fully vegetarian or vegan diet isn't free from the cruelty of farming. All the wheat, barley, corn, soy and various other grains and vegetables that are collected with harvesters contribute to the killing of billions of animals every year.[71] The only difference is that omnivores show a lot more reverence for the sacrifice of life by eating the animals they kill. The arrogance of animal rights advocates assuming they know for certain that plant life doesn't feel pain is matched only by the disregard shown by vegetarians and vegans for the suffering of billions of animals for their own selfish agricultural needs.

FUCK STUPID RELATIONSHIP QUESTIONS

Asking your partner whether or not they're cheating is pointless. Girls I date usually feel insecure about our relationship. Not because the women I date aren't gorgeous, talented and funny. They are. It's because I'm more gorgeous, talented and funny. A woman I once dated felt insecure because women flirted with me in public all the time. For months, she'd tap-dance around the issue and ask me questions about where I was going and with whom I was hanging out. She did this without actually stating that she didn't trust me. It was like having a second mother, except for the occasional hand job. The coy insinuations finally came to a head one day when she asked me point-blank if I was cheating on her.

One of the dumbest questions anyone could ever ask their partner is "Are you cheating on me?" I told her as much. The conversation went like this:

"That's a stupid question."

"Why?"

"Think about it: If I'm cheating on you, that means I'm a duplicitous character. I'd be breaking the premise of a committed relationship, which is trust and honesty, right?"

"Right . . ."

"So if I was cheating on you, that means I'd be a dishonest person, and if I'm dishonest, I'm going to answer 'no.' That's what dishonest people do, they lie."

"Okay . . ."

". . . and if I'm honestly not cheating on you, I'm still going to answer 'no.' Either way, I'm always going to answer that question with 'no.' You can't ever really know for sure if I'm cheating on you, unless you find evidence, which I know you don't have."

That ended the conversation, and we never fought again because girls love being proven wrong with strong, logically sound rebuttals with ambiguous resolutions. She apologized and took me to Disneyland to make up for it. I stayed home because I hate lines, and I had one of the best days of my life playing video games by myself.

She seemed a bit cranky later and asked me whether or not I considered her special, so I told her I thought that she was "one in a million." She said, "Aww, thank you!" I told her it wasn't a compliment. She looked confused, so I explained my reasoning: There are approximately 320 million people in the United States, about half of whom are women, so that means that if she were truly one in a million, there are at least 160 more women like her in the United States alone. Considering the world population of roughly 7 billion people, that means there are probably about 3,500 women like her in the world. She thanked me for being such an awesome realist, offered to give me a piggyback ride across a river, and drowned. But the reason I told her wasn't to be a dick. It was to help her cope with the possibility that we'd break up someday (had she survived). Most men are equally replaceable. I'm the exception, of course, but even if you think you've found a really unique partner, he or she probably isn't that unique. In all likelihood, this person is similar to several thousand others in the world.

The people you date just aren't that special, and neither are you.

Whatever unique or interesting tattoos you might have, all your specialized pornography fetishes, your taste in music and your favorite movies and TV shows—they are enjoyed by millions of other people. Whatever weird shit gets you off probably has its own dedicated website with an active forum of people who are all equally embarrassed about it as you. Being part of a minority doesn't make you unique, it makes you not part of a majority. Unimpressively, 49 percent is still a minority.

Spending a few minutes trawling through profiles on dating sites will demonstrate just how mind-numbingly average most people's wants and desires are. Every girl wants a guy who's cultured and who has a sense of humor, good values and the ability to commit. Every guy wants a hot chick who can "hang with the boys" and share a few of his interests and hobbies. Wow, real deep.

People dating often ask each other what they're looking for in a relationship, but this is the wrong question to ask. What we think we want in a relationship often belies what we truly need to make it sustainable. Qualities like good conflict-resolution skills or being able to tolerate each other during the many hours per year we spend circling parking lots looking for spots are woefully underrepresented on these laundry lists of our desires. Everyone loves a good sense of humor, but nobody ever explicitly states the need for their partner to support their career decisions at the other's expense. It's easy to long for a partner who shares your love of sports or video games, but it's hard to communicate the value of a partner who's secure with who they are.

Another stupid relationship question is "Are you considering this a long-term relationship?" Bitch I might be. That depends on a lot of variables that are hard to predict over the course of a lifetime. That'd be like a car salesman asking you if you'd like to keep your car forever. If a car runs, is reliable, has good gas mileage and performs and looks like new, why wouldn't you? But if it has over-bearing in-laws, co-dependency issues, jealousy or manipulative or abusive tendencies, it's probably time for a trade-in.

FUCK HARD DECISIONS

A coin is the rational thinker's best friend. After considering both sides of a difficult decision, flip a coin. You're welcome.

FUCK CAPTCHAS

How has proving that we're human become such a routine part of life? Computer scientists, systems engineers and user-experience designers spend countless hours every year trying to devise novel ways to test whether a user visiting a website is a human or a bot. Every time I'm tested, I feel like my core identity as part of my species is being called into question. This makes me feel insecure because what if, someday, I'm not able to pass?

All of our responses to CAPTCHA (Completely Automated Public Turing Tests to tell Computers and Humans Apart) on websites, which require us to decipher garbled text or audio, are getting logged somewhere, if only for analytics. If artificial intelligence were ever to become advanced enough to pass these tests, then automated systems looking for "real" humans based on databases of CAPTCHA results may determine that AI is more human than we are. It's a slippery slope into the obsolescence of our species, and it's already happening. Every false negative is a human failing to prove that he or she is human. There may come a day when the majority of humans fail similarly, and we will have tested ourselves out of meaningful existence.

The Turing Test part of the acronym refers to a test conceived by computer scientist and mathematician Alan Turing. It tests a machine's ability to prove that it's human. Turing contended that a machine will pass his "imitation test" if, after interrogation, any person testing the machine will have at most a 70 percent chance of correctly identifying it as a machine after five minutes of conversation.[72] The CAPTCHA tests are like the reverse of a Turing Test, since computers are testing humans. By agreeing to these tests, we're ceding to computers the authority to determine our very humanity, which is itself dehumanizing.

Some variants of CAPTCHA tests ask users logic questions that are designed with the aptitude of a seven-year-old child in mind.[73] For example, a typical question might be "Which is largest amongst a bird, cat and a horse?" Predictably, when testing a logic-based system for registration on the BBC's website, they found that their users felt that these tests were patronizing. Overall, "extremely negative feelings were expressed towards CAPTCHA technology."[74] That's because these systems are patronizing. And they piss off geniuses like me. Casey Henry, an independent marketing analyst, looked at the effect of implementing CAPTCHAs on over fifty different websites over the course of a six-month period (three months with implementation and three without). He found that with no systems in place, spam accounted for 4.1 percent of conversions to his websites. With CAPTCHA in place, that number jumped to 7.3 percent, meaning that roughly 3.2 percent of the humans going to his website were failing the test and therefore not converting.[75] So websites that condescend to humans with these tests are potentially losing almost as many conversions as the number of fake account registrations they're preventing.

In 2013 a company named Vicarious developed technology that could solve text-based CAPTCHA tests 90 percent of the time.[76] When it comes to actual humans, a large-scale Stanford study found that any three-person group of subjects presented with the same image-based CAPTCHA agreed with the result only 71 percent of the time.[77] And audio CAPTCHAs fared even worse, with any three-person agreement test matching only 31 percent of the time. Take a moment to stew over the full implications of these numbers. Computers are now able to pass tests made to determine if a user is human with a higher degree of accuracy than actual humans. This is some *Blade Runner* bullshit that I'm not ready for.

FUCK ENVIRONMENTALISTS

Environmentalists are one of the few activist groups that pisses off its own adherents as much as they piss off nonadherents. It's truly incredible, if you think about it: Environmentalists are fundamentally well intentioned, yet their zeal for their cause and their need to appear to be doing "more than" creates a toxic atmosphere that makes even the people who share their values resent them.

I once rode my bicycle to a grocery store. There, a clipboard activist—someone who stands outside a business and nags patrons for signatures to support a cause—asked me if I was interested in supporting Greenpeace. I promptly and happily said, "No," as I loaded the basket on my bike with groceries. Her face soured. Next, she asked another customer leaving the store the same thing. The second customer said, "No thanks, but I support your cause!" and then opened the door to her hybrid vehicle. The clipboard jockey said, "Thanks for driving a clean car!" Clean *car*? There's no car on Earth cleaner than a bike. Yet because I didn't give lip service to her cause, there was no acknowledgment of this fact. I received no credit, not so much as a thank you or a knowing wink that I was the better person. Nothing.

I was the real hero in that situation. Yet environmental zealots like Greenpeace activists don't seem to care, unless you also support their cult. Their concern for the environment is secondary to the degree to which you support them. This is an activist group that, in 2014, irreparably damaged ancient Peruvian Nazca Lines while, ironically, trying to raise awareness for environmental preservation.[78] The Peruvian lines are geoglyphs created by digging grooves into the ground, and they were built between the years 500 B.C. and A.D. 500.[79] The message that Greenpeace felt was important enough to wreck ancient formations? The trite motto of disingenuous Internet activists everywhere: "Time for Change." The message was to coincide with a UN talk on climate change. Instead of bolstering the cause of climate change activists, they created a noisy diversion by adding some millennials' footprints to an archaeological treasure with a history that's literally millennial.

I regularly do more for the environment than many self-proclaimed activists and planetary caretakers. On a daily basis, I produce nearly no garbage, ride my bike everywhere, do my laundry in large, efficient loads, recycle just about everything and use very little water to cook or clean because I'm spotless. If an outside observer were to view my lifestyle for a few months, he or she might conclude that I was an environmentalist. But rather than receiving knob-shines from a queue of hot lady eco-babes, all I receive is their endless scorn and derision because I happen to call out their stance as overly pious and hypocritical.

I once got scorn from a friend for not recycling a candy wrapper. I told her that my stance on recycling was that if it was convenient, I'd do it. I happened to be standing next to a trash can rather than a recycling bin, so I did a quick mental cost-vs.-benefit calculation. I concluded that the potential benefit of recycling one wrapper would be offset by the energy it would take for me to (A) walk across the room to dispose of it properly and (B) care. In the grand scheme of things, the wrapper has a statistically negligible impact on the environment. Yet this self-proclaimed environmentalist opted to guilt me, instead of picking the wrapper up and disposing of it "properly" herself. Therein lies the problem with most environmentalists: Their desire to recycle and conserve isn't as great as their desire to seem better-than. It's not about the end goal of keeping Earth clean and sustainable but, rather, the tit-for-tat one-upmanship of seeming virtuous. If caring for the environment is a virtue, then he who seems to care the most is deemed to be the most virtuous. But caring, like "awareness," doesn't do things—action does.

The bigger reason I don't care much about the environment is because anyone who has a basic understanding of astronomy knows that Earth is objectively doomed. With or without human intervention, the sun will eventually spend all of its hydrogen fuel and slowly cool down, expanding to the size of a red giant and consuming Earth and everything we love with it. Every single car, building, toy, plant, mountain and, especially, recycle bin will be consumed by our fiery sun. The timeline for this to occur is approximately a billion years, but the so-called habitable zone, where Earth's orbit resides, will be gone long before that, resulting in the complete evaporation of our oceans.[80]

Even if you want to dismiss this concern due to its astronomical timeline, scientists have predicted a number of cataclysmic doomsday events. These range from an asteroid impact to a volcanic apocalypse and even gamma ray bursts, which are exceedingly difficult to predict but a probabilistic certainty over a long enough period of time.[81] Basically, we don't know when Earth will go, but we do know one thing for sure: It *will* go eventually. No amount of picking candy wrappers out of garbage bins will prevent this inevitable conclusion, and any delay we could actuate would be negligible.

Sustainability Is a Red Herring

I want to use everything on Earth as much as I can. I'd like to eat a bison burger while riding a mechanical bull on top of a coal-powered, stretch-M1 Abrams tank through a nest of spotted owls on my way to a party in a very remote, air-conditioned castle. Earth is my oyster, and I will consume it for all it's worth and toss out the shell when I'm done. Because the alternative is destruction at the hands of nature, and nature is abjectly indifferent to joy, suffering, or industry. Unlike a rowdy party guest, nature wrecks entire cities with tornadoes and hurricanes, without leaving behind so much as an amusing tale of drunken debauchery or some trophy panties hanging on the ceiling fan. Only corpses and rubble. Boring.

When we exploit Earth, naturally we should do it in a way that increases humanity's ability to survive. For example, if we mine Earth's resources to build materials to make a space colony, then we should mine Earth to its fullest extent. We should make sure that space colony is the best it can be, to guarantee our survival and future procreation. We should do what it takes to keep this ball spinning in relative stability for as long as it takes for us to ditch it. Earth has no loyalty to us, and we shouldn't have any loyalty to Earth. Basically, my planetary allegiance is an extension of my national allegiance: Just because we were born here doesn't mean we owe it something. We didn't choose where to be born.

FUCK BABY TALK

Baby talk is stupid. Why not treat your child like an adult, so he or she doesn't grow up to be a moron? Or so he or she, at the very least, grows up at all. Some people think it's cute and endearing to derhotacize and replace every *r* with a *w*,* but it makes me clench my butthole with anxiety.

The most obvious reason parents do this with children is that they want to be relatable. Babies "speak" in babble, with malformed words and sentences, and parents are too blinded by their love for their kids to realize that they're speaking like morons. But if someone visited China and started speaking in a heavy, condescending Asian accent, people would think that guy was an asshole. You wouldn't go to Great Britain and present your best caricature of a wigged barrister to seem relatable, so why would you do the equivalent with a child?

Also, why do it specifically with language? Parents don't revert to a state of incompetence, in which they aren't able to drive, prepare food, walk or bathe themselves to become more

---

* Also known as *R*-labialization, popularized by idiot babies and the Looney Tunes character Elmer Fudd, who pronounces words like "rabbit" as "wabbit." Stupid.

relatable. What kind of message does this send to kids? Do you think children respect you more or less when you come down to their level?

I once went to a friend's house and she gave me her baby to hold, in spite of my protestation. She went into the kitchen for what seemed like minutes and left me alone with her kid, so I decided to have a conversation with her baby. In a normal but stern tone, I spoke to him about how fast I can drive, my typing speed and which companies had the most promising new technology at this year's Consumer Electronics Show. It was the worst conversation I've ever had. The idiot just stared at me. Had I lowered myself to his level, his side of that conversation would have gone exactly the same, but I'd have looked and felt like an idiot.

What's worse is when people do this with animals—especially dogs. At least when humans speak to other humans, there's a remote possibility that one of these children is a genius who will be able to communicate in some substantial way. Animals don't understand our language, culture, social norms or facial cues. No amount of high-rising "upspeak" will make a dog more comprehending because they are animals that eat their own shit. Even on the off chance that a dog does recognize certain human facial tics after years of associating human behavioral cues with rewards of snacks, I'm not going to be impressed by any animal that can be fooled by pretending to throw a tennis ball and not letting go. I've never been fooled in such a manner.

Dogs, babies and children aren't on my level. I'm not going to stoop to theirs to seem more relatable. It's beneath me. It's beneath us all. If you like babies, the most respectful thing you can do is treat them like adults. They'll appreciate you for it when they grow up. Nobody wants to be talked down to "like a child," and that phrase has negative connotations for a reason. Isn't it about time we cut the bullshit and started expecting our babies and animals to rise to our level of discourse instead of us having to lower ourselves to theirs?

FUCK PARENTS WHO DON'T
WANT MY PARENTING ADVICE

I know what it takes to raise a baby because I used to be one. Every single parent friend of mine always whines about how hard it is, but to me it seems like the easiest job in the world. If you don't end up killing your child due to neglect, you've already got a huge leg up on the competition.* Not killing a baby is easy: All you have to do is feed it once a day, make sure it doesn't eat anything stupid and rotate its sleeping position every now and then so it doesn't atrophy. Done.

Being a good parent is all about being efficient. I'd be the best parent in the world because I know how to take shortcuts when taking care of things. For example, I once bought a houseplant and kept it alive for three months. I did it by creating a custom planter so every time I watered it, the excess water that wasn't trapped by the soil would collect in a basin, eliminating the need for a tacky drip-plate. Every time you water a plant it strips some nutrients from the soil, so rather than wasting it by pouring it out, I'd pour the water back on the plant when it was time to water it again. If you have multiple plants, you can cycle the water source

---

* The competition being all other parents. Every parent is in an unspoken competition with every other parent to have the baddest son or daughter on the block.

among them to give a greater variety of nutrients to each plant. People can't help but gush praise on me when they learn of my technique. This praise is wasted on me because I already know it's ingenious, and I'm too busy reaching around my shoulder to pat myself on the back to care.

Similarly, when it comes to a baby, I'd find time-saving measures like a netted papoose. I could hang the baby around my neck while I shower and have the runoff soap wash the baby simultaneously. If the baby gets tired, he or she could fall asleep while I shower and I wouldn't have to worry about my idiot baby sticking a fork in the socket while I wasn't watching him, which would be often. And speaking of sockets, I'd create special low-voltage decoy outlets in my house and intentionally allow my baby to put his or her fingers in them. These outlets would shock the baby with a much lower voltage than a regular outlet, teaching my child a valuable lesson while simultaneously being safe for the child. It'd save me years of having to worry or explain to my child the dangers of being a dipshit. I could then put that surplus time to use enlightening other parents on how to be better at raising their children.

Food is another gross inefficiency when it comes to child-rearing: namely, giving your children a choice in the food they eat. Kids are fickle and naive when it comes to eating. Their decision-making process is one big confirmation bias based on their limited dining experiences. They don't know what they want to eat any more than they know what kind of luxury automobile they want to drive. When it comes to food, a child's opinion is either worthless or, at best, uninformed. So it's doubly frustrating to watch parents waste everyone's time by asking their kids to choose something from a menu in a busy restaurant. Servers are in a hurry, and there are other paying customers who know what they want.

They are adults who can read and have bank accounts, mortgages and lives to lead. When you have a teaching moment with your child, meandering about the menu, enunciating every word and describing flavors to your little spawn, those busy people don't find it as cute as you do.

What do you as a parent have to say about food anyway? Probably jack shit. In all likelihood you aren't even a writer by trade, since most people aren't. The adjectives you use to describe the flavors are going to be inadequate, incorrect or both. We've all got shit to do, so why don't you do everyone—including your child—a favor and order for him? Kids are easy to feed: You give them food and they eat it. If they won't, then they can learn a very valuable lesson in starvation. The pangs of hunger will soon turn into tears of regret, which will teach them yet another thing: Tears taste salty! Children should eat what you give them, and that's that. My parents had one thing for dinner every night, and that was food. If I didn't like it, my other option was no food. I learned quickly that some food was better than no food, so I ate what I was served. If I added up all the time over the course of my life I've spent in restaurants waiting for kids to order, it'd easily be tens of minutes. I could have used that time wrestling Bolivian Cholitas Luchadoras. Hell yeah.

FUCK THE EIGHTH AMENDMENT

The Eigth amendment of the United States Constitution states: "Excessive bail shall not be required, nor excessive fines imposed, nor cruel and unusual punishments inflicted." It's like a hot dog that starts out great, but the last bite is dry, shitty bread. Cruel and unusual punishments are not only compatible with a fair and just society, but they could actually enhance civilization. Punishments should be unusual, if only as a testament to society's ingenuity. People in every profession are allowed some degree of self-expression, even in seemingly technical fields like computer science and engineering. Programmers of NASA's Apollo 11 mission left behind witty commentary and cultural references in their code, even though they didn't expect anyone to read it.[82] So why do we deny executioners the same right to express themselves? And is it necessary to add insult to injury by explicitly stating it in a country's most fundamental doctrine of law?

The more unusual a penalty, the better. We already know what doesn't work: everything we've been doing. The word "incorrigible" is an adjective used to describe someone who's impervious to correction by punishment, and likely it came into use right around the time our forefathers approved the notion that punishments should be routine. A death penalty that has become so prosaic that it elicits no emotion in the executioner makes us all slightly less human. One should feel something when taking a life or inflicting pain. When that process becomes as mundane as flipping a switch, it disassociates us from our personhood and turns us into task-completing automatons. Even parrots can complete simple tasks, like pulling levers for treats. Except the "treat" here is diminished returns on a threadbare execution method. Society's punishments have become so boring that executioners are themselves at risk of dying from boredom.

The solution to this existential dread is to be creative with our punishments. Instead of an electric chair, why not an electric rodeo bull? The felon doesn't have to try to stay on, because he or she has no choice. They are strapped in for the ride of their lives . . . or ride *for* their lives. As they sit atop a 2,000-volt mechanical bull, if they can survive thirty seconds while being electrocuted and bucked, they get a new lease on life and a free pair of novelty cowboy spurs. Surviving unusual punishments should beget unusual rewards. If you can outwit or outlast the cleverest executioner, you get a second chance at life and a small prize.

There are typically only four methods currently used for execution. They are:

Lethal Injection

This is the injection of drugs into a person's circulatory system. The effect is to cause paralysis, unconsciousness and eventual death when the body's organs shut down, starving the brain of oxygen.

The Problem: Too creepy; there's something unsettling about slowly putting a needle into someone. You're a human, not a mosquito. Plus if they miss your vein while injecting you, they may need to prick you multiple times until they get it right, which can be very annoying.

Better Alternative: *Lethal Ejection.* The felon is placed atop a commercial airliner in a capsule that is launched into the atmosphere along with the lavatory contents. No parachute, just a capsule filled with one hardened criminal and a bunch of hardened turds, launched over the Atlantic while commercial passengers sleep quietly below, dreaming of their family vacations.

The Reward: If you survive the impact, you are gifted the ejection capsule, in which to start a new life in whatever desert or ocean you land in.

The Electric Chair

The condemned person is strapped into a wooden chair and electrocuted through conductors attached to the person's head and legs.

The Problem: It's boring. A powerful jolt of electricity is said to disable the brain, but that's only if the boredom of using this method doesn't do it first.

Better Alternative: *The Hall of Vending.* The felon is sent down a long hallway full of wobbly vending machines that may tip at any moment, instantly crushing the captive. The convict is kept from food or drink for several days prior to the run, and one vending machine at the end of the hallway contains a bag of chips that the prisoner can obtain for a small sum of change. Each vending machine along the way may have a few coins sitting on the top shelf inside the machine that the prisoner has to shake to obtain. Each ensuing vending machine will be heavier and wobblier. If he or she obtains enough change, they will encounter the final machine containing the bag of chips—but the chips remain stuck at the top and need to be shaken free in a final feat of strength and hubris.

The Reward: Chips.

Hanging

Nooses are hung around people's necks, and those people are dropped from some height. They either asphyxiate, or the noose breaks their neck.

The Problem: You can't hang anyone in a room without ceilings that are adequately high. In which case, you'll need a ladder, rope, stepping stool for the condemned to stand on (temporarily) and shears to cut them down. It's equal parts execution and supermarket sweep at the hardware store.

Better Alternative: *Pie Cyclone.* You sit on a carnival ride that spins you around at high speed. As the cyclone picks up speed, clowns pie you in the face repeatedly. If a convict can survive being pied in the face hundreds of times in fifteen minutes on the cyclone without asphyxiation, he or she gets a second chance at life.

The Reward: You can eat the leftover pie stuck to your clothing and hair, plus take any unused execution pies—a welcome addition to most backyard barbecues.

Firing Squad

The felon experiences Newton's First Law of Motion firsthand with his or her skull.

The Problem: Firing squads are like the vanilla ice cream of executions: It's always an option, nobody is excited about it and anyone who settles for it is disappointed.

Better Alternative: *Cheese Fondue–boarding.* Like water-boarding, except with hot cheddar. Dinner guests will dip skewers of bread and fruit in the sauce while they discuss inane topics like lucid dreaming and how we are all connected. If drowning in hot cheese doesn't kill the felon, the deadly dull conversation might.

The Reward: A chocolate fondue–boarding. Yum!

Society has innovated on the fronts of education, healthcare and technology; isn't it about time we innovated on the penalty front?

FUCK SOULMATES

Thinking you have a soulmate—your one and only true love, that one person who understands you more than anyone else—is a curse. First, the concept is devastating to widows and widowers. If your soulmate dies or it doesn't work out for whatever reason, you will think you have lost your only shot at happiness. You'll be left doubting the most important decision you've ever made in your life. And why should we be burdened with making that decision? Most people have trouble picking a cell phone or TV that works reliably, and that's with the benefit of consumer reviews, product specifications, and in-store testing.

Yet somehow, without any prior experience or qualitative metrics to compare, we're supposed to be able to suss out our one and only. People meet their "soulmates" all the time, and they're sure of their decision right up until they aren't. Sometimes relationships end not because the partners have changed but because they finally see each other for who they really are: petty, manipulative and otherwise awful people who lack emotional maturity and depth. Or maybe the differences are as mundane as a lack of common interests. Or maybe the relationship ended due to boredom, distance or competing romantic interests.

Whatever the case, the moment we decide we've found our soulmate—and let's not kid ourselves, it is a decision—we hold those beliefs to be true only until we make the opposite decision. It happens astonishingly frequently, to the tune of about 50 percent of married people.[83] It's relatively safe to assume that most people, outside those marrying to commit immigration or insurance fraud, choose to marry because they believe they've found their soulmates. Yet roughly half of these people turn out to be wrong. Think about it: Half of the people you meet will be wrong about one of the most important decisions they will ever make.

The concept of a soulmate is especially onerous to widows and widowers. They're the unfortunate few who don't get to see their relationships through to their natural conclusions: double hip replacement and adult diapers. The bereaved were likely just as fallible as the general populace at choosing their soulmates, so the odds that their relationship would have ended due to divorce were still one in two. Only now they lack the benefit of certainty due to the untimely departure of their spouse. The only thing incrementally less tragic than losing a spouse is losing a spouse you were destined to divorce. It's similar to the difference between getting fired and getting fired from a job you eventually would have quit.

The contemporary Western concept of a "soulmate" can be traced to 350 B.C., approximately when Plato wrote *The Symposium*. In it, Plato recounts a story by the ancient Greek playwright Aristophanes. It's about humanity's origins, involving some bizarre theory of ancient humans having eight limbs and two faces.[84] The full description is so full of wacky bullshit, it has to be read verbatim to be appreciated:

The primeval man was round, his back and sides forming a circle; and he had four hands and four feet, one head with two faces, looking opposite ways, set on a round neck and precisely alike; also four ears, two privy members, and the remainder to correspond. He could walk upright as men now do, backwards or forwards as he pleased, and he could also roll over and over at a great pace, turning on his four hands and four feet, eight in all, like tumblers going over and over with their legs in the air; this was when he wanted to run fast.

—Aristophanes, *The Symposium*, 350 B.C.

This early human was, for all intents and purposes, a sentient bowling ball. I asked my illustrator to draw what she thought this creature would look like based on Aristophanes's description. Here's what she came up with (Fig. 20).

Fig. 20: This abomination is the alleged origin of humanity.

Aristophanes goes on to tell a yarn about how this ancient creature rose up against the gods, who punished it by splitting it into two halves. They had to be sewn up and formed into separate beings by the Greek god Apollo, who's likened to a cobbler. "He also moulded the breast and took out most of the wrinkles," Aristophanes claims, "much as a shoemaker might smooth leather upon a last." Then he caps it off with this corny prose about how the two halves long for each other and that each half is always looking for the other:

> **And the reason is that human nature was originally one and we were a whole, and the desire and pursuit of the whole is called love. There was a time, I say, when we were one, but now because of the wickedness of mankind God has dispersed us.**
> **—Aristophanes, *The Symposium*, 350 B.C.**

Yes, the modern concept of "soulmate" comes from an ancient Greek man who thought our ancestors had four ears and traveled by somersault. In other words, our romantic concept of love comes from a liar. Either that, or an idiot. But let's not discount the possibility that he was both.

Yet despite this ludicrous origin, people still shackle themselves with the burden of finding their other half, which sets us up for failure. By choosing soulmates, people are essentially making lifelong bets on other people, without any rational reason for choosing or reasonable expectation of success. In the stock market there's a word for people who invest without assurance or reason: bankrupt. It's also a concept that relies upon *exceptional arrogance*.

The other problem with the concept of a soulmate is that it relies on time and space. If a soulmate is to exist, he or she must exist in the same century and decade as you, otherwise what's the point? And not only must you exist at the same time, the difference in age can be at most twenty or thirty years in order to have a legal or compatible sexual relationship. And then, against all odds, that person has to happen to live in the same location as you. The satirical website *The Onion* published an article in 2002 titled "18-Year-Old Miraculously Finds Soulmate in Hometown." It underlines the statistical absurdity of the hope of finding your "soulmate" in the city you were born in. The article describes a fictional boy who finds himself astonished that, despite having only left his hometown twice in his life, "both times for marching-band competitions," he was able to find his one and only true love, "in a town of only 3,400 people."

Even if you're one of the sappy idiots who still believes in the notion of a soulmate, the odds of you finding yours isn't in your favor, especially if you've never traveled outside your country. In fact, from a purely probabilistic standpoint, your soulmate is likely of Chinese or Indian descent, being that about three in eight people are of either origin. The United States makes up roughly only 4.5 percent of the world's population, so there's a 95 percent chance that your soulmate won't be American and probably doesn't even speak the same language as you. Most people aren't financially solvent enough to travel the world in search of this missing other half. And let's face it, the person you drunkenly hooked up with from your local bar, or your high school sweetheart you met in third period English class, probably isn't your predestined missing half. It's just someone you're banging out of convenience and proximity.

Let's not bring divine intervention into this. You're hooking up with someone you find attractive enough to tolerate. You weren't destined by some cosmic force to grind your genitals together. No otherworldly force gives a shit about you enough to make sure you get laid semiregularly. It's this exceptional arrogance that makes people depressed when they don't fulfill this arbitrary relationship standard. Widows and widowers have it hard enough—let's not pile on the unrealistic possibility that the person they lost was uniquely qualified to make them happy. Fuck soulmates.

FUCK PEOPLE WHO ARE AFRAID
OF LIGHTNING AND THUNDER

Anyone who is afraid of lightning and thunder is an idiot. Being a child or house pet is no excuse. I'm not afraid of lightning and thunder, because I know they are common, relatively safe occurrences in nature—plus I'm a grizzled hardass who's certain he could survive a lightning strike. Any person or animal afraid of lightning doesn't understand probability and isn't worthy of keeping my company. The number of people who die from lightning strikes every year in the United States is approximately thirty-one.[85] You're more than twice as likely to be killed by a lawn mower, about ten times more likely to drown in a bathtub and fourteen times more likely to die falling out of bed.[86] Yet nobody is afraid of a bed. In fact, it's what people jump into for safety when they hear thunder—ironically increasing their risk of death manyfold.

Ever see a cow during a thunderstorm? It acts like a total moron, hysterical, running around and colliding into trees, until finally knocking itself dead. That's all there is to say about cows and lightning.

FUCK TRIGGER WARNINGS

Trigger warnings are about the people making them, not the survivors of trauma. They are meant to be a warning to people who've suffered trauma, usually rape—that what they're about to read, watch, or listen to may trigger some post-traumatic stress. It's a hollow gesture that ends up doing the exact opposite of what's intended, because the very act of mentioning to a sexual assault victim that they might be reminded of their sexual assault is *reminding them of their sexual assault.*

Reading the words "trigger warning" suggests that there's some content to follow that might trigger an episode. It makes it impossible for abuse victims to forget about their violation and live normal lives, without constant and overt reminders that they've been victimized. When a rape victim reads something in context that may trigger a post-traumatic event, he or she will have one of the two following reactions: either they will be reminded of their traumatic event or they won't. By explicitly reminding them of their traumatic event out of context, you're eliminating the possibility that they could have read the material without being affected. They no longer have the option of not associating material with their own history, as you have made that choice for them.

Although these warnings are usually done with seemingly good intentions, it's astoundingly condescending to rape victims. It's a little reminder that they will always be victims, and that they should consume all media through the lens of that victimhood. People who post trigger warnings are making the patronizing assumption that rape victims need to be coddled with topical safety nets. Jennifer,* a rape victim I interviewed for this book, said that these warnings weren't prevalent around the time of her assault in 2005. If they had been, she doesn't think they would have been helpful. When it comes to PTSD, what you need is "professional help, not trigger warnings," Jennifer said. She contends that with PTSD, "anything can be a trigger." She recalls that watching the movie *Anchorman: The Legend of Ron Burgundy*, a 2004 comedy about a San Diego news anchor, triggered her. In a 2013 study published in the journal *Science*, neuroscientists at Rutgers University found that mice who received a small shock simultaneously with the release of a specific odor showed heightened sensitivity to that fear-inducing odor, even before the threatening message was sent to the brain. "We know that anxiety disorders like PTSD can sometimes be triggered by smell, like the smell of diesel exhaust for a soldier," says John McGann, associate professor in the Department of Psychology and contributing author to the study.[87]

Stacy, a friend of mine who has been the victim of a sexual assault, agrees. The prevalence of these warnings in media hasn't helped people like her and Jennifer avoid any potentially "triggering" material. What it has done is create the unintended side effect of reminding her of her victimization, even when she had no intention of reading or watching the offending section of assigned

---

* Names changed to protect anonymity.

coursework in the first place. For example, not all literature in academia is meant to be consumed entirely, as professors often focus on certain chapters or sections as part of a greater lesson or study. A trigger warning before a literary work may remind victims of their trauma, even in instances where they had no intention of reading the potentially offending excerpt.

What's worse is that now college campuses are being encouraged by advocacy groups to include trigger warnings in college textbooks and required reading material for the curriculum. In 2013, Oberlin College published a guideline for its faculty suggesting that books like Chinua Achebe's *Things Fall Apart* contain trigger warnings for anyone who may have experienced "racism, colonialism, religious persecution, violence, suicide and more."[88] The guide goes on to patronizingly remind us that students "have lives before and outside [the] classroom," and that an instructor's earnest desire to avoid "spoiling" a text isn't reason enough not to issue a trigger warning. "Even if a trigger warning does contain a spoiler, experiencing a trigger is always, always worse than experiencing a spoiler," the guide states. Further, vague language about material that's "upsetting" isn't enough of a warning and "may sound patronizing."

Indeed.

The policy was widely criticized, and it was temporarily shelved, pending further review. This kind of policy has far-reaching implications and may lead to a chilling effect on free speech. One of the beautiful things about literature is that authors are not inhibited from expressing themselves in their writing. Books have no rating system or regulatory overreach from organizations such as the Entertainment Software Rating Board (ESRB), Record Industry Association of America (RIAA), or the Motion Picture Association of America (MPAA). Before the motion picture rating system was instituted in 1968, the public put pressure on the government to oversee what Hollywood was and wasn't allowed to release.[89] To avoid inconsistent regulations and governmental overreach—which might be much more stringent than self-imposed regulation—the motion picture industry decided to create a regulatory body to police itself. The result is the system we have now, ranging from G for general audiences to PG and PG-13 for parental guidance and R for age restricted. There's also the rarely issued and infamous NC-17 rating, which strictly prohibits younger audiences from viewing movies with strong adult themes, nudity and extreme violence.

The NC-17 rating usually spells financial doom for films. Now that the entertainment market has been splintered, movies aren't as profitable as they used to be. Video games, websites, online videos, podcasts and social networking are taking up a larger share of audiences' free time. Studios are reluctant to produce films with an age-restricted rating because of limited distribution, merchandising and marketing opportunities. That's why classic R-rated movies from the 1980s like *Robocop* and *Die Hard* have had millennial reboots that were rated PG-13. Even movies based on violent literature, like *World War Z,* have been censored by studios to obtain that coveted PG-13 rating. The book version of *World War Z* had graphic depictions of zombies being decapitated and humans having their limbs ripped apart. The movie adaptation showed almost no gore and was a tepid piece of shit. Audiences rated the movie only 67 percent on the movie-review website Rotten Tomatoes, whereas the uncensored book received an 84 percent positive score on Amazon. In a climactic scene in the movie, as a zombie's head gets bashed in, the camera pans off-screen. It gave me violence blue-balls. After the movie, I slammed my car door shut on my hand a few times, just so I could feel some relief.

Just as movie ratings rein in risqué film content, trigger warnings in literature could have the exact same effect on books. Semantics aside, these trigger warnings are functionally the same as film ratings; acts of violence, sexual assault, kidnapping, or hate crimes are listed up-front and center. They warn not just victims of sexual assault but anyone who may be concerned about the material they're about to read, such as parents and other advocacy groups. Over time, it may be simpler to give books with content like this a rating system like movies. If a professor assigns books with trigger warnings to his or her class, and students opt not to read these books, to avoid potential trauma, the school administration is left with one of the following options: either not penalize the student for boycotting the offending material, or force the professor to change the required coursework or to provide alternate reading materials. Not penalizing a student for abstaining from coursework leaves the door open for students to abuse the system by making false trauma claims. Forcing the instructor to change or omit the reading material may not always be feasible, as certain authors are studied for specific styles or themes. So that puts pressure on the educator to avoid assigning the potentially offensive material altogether and changing what is taught in schools.

The American Library Association (ALA) has declared labeling a "censor's tool." They fundamentally oppose the practice because it may serve as a means to "prejudice people's attitudes toward library resources."[90] In a Q&A section on the ALA website, it's explicitly stated that ratings systems are a violation of the Library Bill of Rights:[91]

These rating systems are devised by private groups using subjective and changing criteria to advise people of suitability or content of materials. It is the library's responsibility to prevent the imposition or endorsement of private rating systems. Including such ratings in the bibliographic record, library records and other library-authored finding aids would predispose people's attitudes toward the material and thus violate the Library Bill of Rights.

—American Library Association, July 2015

Another staunch opponent of such labeling is the American Association of University Professors (AAUP). It's a nonprofit organization founded in 1915 to make sure that higher-education institutions don't violate norms of academic freedom and governance. The AAUP is opposed to trigger warnings in academia, stating that trigger warnings "run the risk of reducing complex literary, historical, sociological and political insights to a few negative characterizations."[92] In a 2014 AAUP report, they issued the following rebuke of the practice:

A trigger warning might . . . elicit a response from students they otherwise would not have had, focusing them on one aspect of a text and thus precluding other reactions. If, for example, *The House of Mirth* or *Anna Karenina* carried a warning about suicide, students might overlook the other questions about wealth, love, deception and existential anxiety that are what those books are actually about.

—American Association of University Professors, August 2014

Book publishers rely on the sales of books assigned to students as part of a curriculum. Academic book sales can make up a significant portion of a book's profits. If educators appeased advocacy groups by not assigning literature with trigger warnings, it would make those books less profitable, which would discourage publishers from publishing, and writers from writing, potentially offensive literature. This self-censorship would create a pallid book-publishing industry fraught with literature that's safe, unchallenging and dishonest. In short, it would suck as much as the movie industry.

This isn't just slippery-slope alarmism. The groundwork for these policies has already begun to take place. In 2014, the University of California, Santa Barbara (UCSB), student government passed a resolution to "mandate warnings for triggering content in academic settings."[93] The student bill contends that "Trigger Warnings should be used for content not covered by the rating system used by the MPAA or TV warnings (such as contains violence, nudity or, language [sic])," and that instructors should "not dock points from a student's overall grade for being absent or leaving class early if the reason for the absence is the triggering content."

Yet in the rush to issue warnings on classic or contemporary works of literature, it raises the question:

Who's going to write all these trigger warnings?

Someone has to read all these books, right? If trigger warnings are necessary to help trauma victims avoid further trauma, and the prevalence of trauma is so ubiquitous that we need universal trigger warnings, then presumably a significant number of people who are tasked with reading these books to find potential triggers are themselves victims of traumatic experiences. Is it fair for us to expect anyone to endure potentially triggering material, if we can't even expect students in an academic setting to abide this possible discomfort? Should we ask potential proofreaders to disclose any sexual, racial, colonial or gendered trauma they may have experienced before a potential work assignment? Is it fair to expect proofreaders at publishing houses to endure psychological anguish, or should we start including a questionnaire for prospective proofreaders, editors, designers, lawyers and countless other people who may encounter this material during the publishing process, to disclose their mental health status before every task? Where do our efforts to protect people end and the harsh realities of life—that sometimes we have to endure uncomfortable situations—begin?

Even if employees were asked to disclose this information, it would be a legal minefield for publishers. They would have to contend with various healthcare privacy acts in different countries. Not to mention a huge liability for publishers who may be tasked with not just keeping their employees' healthcare records private, but to do an accurate, representative and consistent job of disclosing potentially triggering material. It's not a stretch of the imagination to foresee lawsuits from customers who may feel that the warnings preceding a text were inadequate. This would create a demand for standardized warning criteria or, at the very least, a legal disclaimer prepending books. The governing body regulating that criteria will likely come from one of two sources: industry or government. And as we've seen with the movie industry, even self-governance ends up overreaching and leads to self-censorship.

There's only one real solution to this dilemma: force authors to include trigger warnings in their own writing, before it even gets to the publisher. That way, the onus is on the writer to be sensitive to all possible concepts and scenarios that could induce memories of traumatic events. Let's pass legislation that forces authors to take sensitivity courses to become familiar with not just issues dealing with racism, sexism, classism and sexual orientation, but war, violence, disabilities, illnesses, death, molestation, drugs, authoritarianism, inmate trauma and all phobias, so that no one, not even the publisher, will ever get surprised with a potential trigger ever again.

FUCK PEOPLE WHO
AGREE WITH YOU

Having people agree with you makes you reaffirm your opinions. You think you're correct, because it seems like you're in the majority. Of course, where this dynamic falls short is when your beliefs are terrible—such as being racist, bigoted or otherwise prejudiced. The constant stream of validation we all receive on social media from our friends and "followers," coupled with the homogeneous echo chamber of like-minded opinions, creates an iron bubble of bad ideas, reinforced by dumbasses.

For example, here's a scenario: Someone has a loud, polarizing opinion and decides to share that opinion on a social network. Normally, that opinion will provoke dissent from people who disagree, creating a healthy debate that may lead to a greater understanding for a handful of people. Where this process breaks down is when the original poster (OP) adds a caveat that his opinion needs no further qualification and either asks dissenters to "unfriend" him or her if they disagree, or the OP decides to actively silence dissenting opinions by blocking or removing contradictory comments from the discussion.

The opposing voices and viewpoints disappear, leaving behind only like-minded followers who affirm the original poster's idiotic worldview. This phenomenon is related to the concept of a "filter bubble," a phrase coined by activist and author Eli Pariser, which refers to the algorithmic filtering of opposing beliefs. This self-imposed filter gives the OP the impression that his or her opinions are getting more unanimously popular over time. In reality, the same or greater number of people out there disagree, but the OP has selected them out of the discussion.

It's the rhetorical analog to a Japanese blacksmith folding a katana blade back over itself repeatedly, to make it purer and stronger. Except here the blade being strengthened is an idiotic opinion, purified in a furnace of stupid.

When a famous director has a misfire and creates a movie that's objectively flawed and shitty, people ask "How could something so flawed and shitty make it through so many levels of people without anyone realizing that they were making some grade-A garbage?" The answer, more often than not, is simple: The director surrounded him- or herself with yes-men. When a bad decision is made, not only does it go unchallenged, but he also has the reinforcement of a cadre of idiots, ready to applaud every bad decision. It's an easy trap to fall into upon attaining any level of influence. People who remove dissenting opinions from their professional or political lives find themselves surrounded by people who won't give them an honest opinion. They are either afraid of losing their jobs, like in the case of the director, or they lack perspective and objectivity due to being too close to the source and being lost in his or her cult of celebrity.

Early in my writing career, I wrote an article on my website where I criticized the "goth" subculture as being silly, disingenuous and homogenized. The culture seemed to be full of people who fancied themselves distinguished and unique but who are easily identifiable due to sharing all the exact same aesthetics, music, lifestyles and interests. Many people commended my article, but the praise wasn't universal.

Upon publishing my opinions, I received a fair amount of backlash from people who identified as being goth. The hate mail I received was angry and poorly written. That was to be expected, as people who are preoccupied first and foremost with the appearance of seeming dark and mysterious tend not to care as much about spelling and grammar. I was curious about the demographics of some of the people emailing me, so I decided to investigate.

One of the hallmarks of my website is that I'd usually look up my critics to see what kind of lives they lead, who they are and why they are criticizing me. For creating a dossier of my haters, my friends gave me the nickname "The Reverse Stalker." There was some legitimacy to this policy, as over the years I'd received a number of threats: violence, sexual assault, death and harm to my family. This was a way to keep tabs on my idiotic and/or obsessed detractors.

In the early days of the Internet, it was relatively easy to investigate the sender of an email, since almost every mail server included the sender's real IP address. An IP address is what identifies your computer uniquely on the Internet and allows websites and servers to route traffic to and from your computer. It was trivial to find someone's approximate location with an IP address geo-location tool. Coupled with search engines and a few other tools, it was often possible to find out a person's real name, home address, personal website, affiliations, place of employment and a lot of other important, embarrassing or otherwise private information. I rarely needed anything other than someone's website to glean insights into his or her thinking and temperament, which was usually the only reason I'd look anyone up.

One person in particular was an adolescent with his own website dedicated to goth art, music and poetry. He delighted in receiving fan mail from other goths who praised his site, which made me realize that his opinions were just like my own—equal in magnitude, only opposite in position. Every element of goth culture I criticized, he heralded. Every aesthetic choice I found boring and mundane, he found unique and interesting. For all intents and purposes, he was the polar opposite of me. With his faux-spooky aesthetic, he was the goth-loving yin to my hateful yang.

The positive response to his website from his followers was similar to the positive response to my website that I received from my followers. There was nothing inherently right or wrong about his praise for the subculture he loved; he was simply expressing an opinion, as was I. Since preferential opinions aren't inherently right or wrong, the only thing separating us was the opinions of our respective fans. His fans were biased toward him because they liked his points of view, and my fans were biased toward me because they liked mine. His love of goth culture was unimpeach-able, but the reason he loved it—the alleged uniqueness—was flawed. His fans were misleading him into believing something about his lifestyle that wasn't true.

It was at that moment I became skeptical of my admirers. I realized that by listening to the praise of my fans, I could just as easily have a skewed perspective of the popularity and merit of my thoughts and opinions. Thankfully, all my opinions are rock-solid, and I've never believed in anything stupid even for a minute.

My skepticism of admirers is part of the reason I've opted on my website to only display email that is critical of me. I realized long ago that most criticism I receive is flawed, lazy, or fallacious, so I take it with a grain of salt. But it was this exchange with the angry goth who helped me realize that, equally, I needed to take my praise with a grain of salt, as usually neither had merit.

Just because someone agrees with you doesn't mean your opinion or perspective is correct. For example, many believe that illegal immigrants are "taking our jobs," but that perspective is myopic and one-sided. Illegal immigrants can't simply "take" a job. Companies must be willing to give them those jobs in the first place (Fig. 21). It shifts the perspective from one of victimization—the belief that "our" assets (in this case, jobs) are being stolen—to one of shared guilt, in which multiple parties are at fault. The latter is the kind of nuanced and evenhanded point of view that's rarely seen in political discourse these days. That's because it's my point of view, and I'm a brilliant and critical thinker.

Fig. 21: Immigrants can't "take our jobs."
Companies offer them those jobs.

FUCK MATERNITY AND PATERNITY LEAVE

There's a growing chorus of people who are bemoaning the lack of standard maternity leave—and, to a lesser extent, paternity leave—in the United States. Proponents argue that people shouldn't have to choose between raising a family and having a career. You don't. You can do both, you just can't do both well. All excellence in life requires focus, to the exclusion of other things.

An insidious side effect of granting maternity and paternity leave is that it discriminates against the childless. The infertile may want children, and now insult is heaped upon injury, as happy fertile parents get six weeks of paid vacation on top of their reproductive success? And what about the people who can't have kids for other reasons? They're too ugly? Their standards are too high? They're homosexuals who, for whatever reason, can't or won't adopt? What about people who have psychological or cognitive disabilities that prevent them from making the lifelong commitment of having a child? What then? Do we simply exclude these people from the pool of benefits allotted to healthy, straight parents who are able and willing to have a child? Do we punish people who can't or won't find a suitable mate?

Either we have to grant everyone the same amount of paid leave, so that nobody is discriminated against; or we must make every baby sign a contract at birth assuring society that he or she will pay back in full all subsidies granted to the parents for being born. It's high time we start holding babies accountable for their unilateral dependence on society. Want to have a baby? Great. Go have one, but make sure it pays back its dues. Nobody should encourage or discourage you with regard to having a baby, although a case can be made that most people should be discouraged, and I'm the right person to make that case.

Having babies is one of the few actions in society where we give people carte blanche to do as they see fit. If you want to raise your child to have terrible taste in cuisine, music and clothing, you're allowed to. You can teach your child all sorts of goofy bullshit in place of science and academics. You can give him or her a discriminatory point of view toward minorities. That's your prerogative. As a society, we've collectively decided not to intervene with any of that.

But why the hell not? Children aren't raised in a bubble. A shitty parent will almost always raise a shitty child, and that shitty child will probably grow up to be a shitty adult—and the next thing you know, you're standing behind some idiot in a restaurant who's loudly reading the menu to his own stupid children, holding up all the hardworking adults unencumbered by children of their own. We can do better than this. We should make potential parents pass an aptitude test before having a child.

The test would be a simple, one-question test with one answer: *Do you think a child should be disciplined?*

The answer is: Yes. No nuance, no theory, no debate. Just a black-and-white affirmation that a kid should be taught that his or her actions have consequences. Those consequences can be anything from a stern talking-to, if you're a pussy; or five across the eyes, if you're old school and Child Protective Services isn't looking. Babies are idiots, and parents seem to tacitly acknowledge this by putting them in cribs with physical barriers to enforce boundaries. But as soon as the baby grows up enough to talk back, some parents opt to remove all boundaries and let the child act like a petulant asshole. That asshole will grow up without the tools to cope with life and will, in all likelihood, also raise kids to become dipshits, and the cycle continues.

Raising children is a huge responsibility, and many people opt out of it. They're intelligent enough to know that they can't successfully balance a work schedule and home life. But rather than acknowledging these people—society's most prudent and responsible members—we're rewarding the impulsivity of the horny, hasty and thoughtless. People who have kids, but who aren't prepared for their entire expense, including unpaid leave and/or the risk of being fired for an elective extended absence, are reckless at best and exploitative at worst. Why reward them?

FUCK RHYMES

People who find meaning in song lyrics, especially rhyming lyrics, are lazy thinkers. They're not readers, scholars, or academics. They're slacker idiots who look to popular music for their life lessons and inspiration. Whether it's college kids who lay around in their dorm rooms listening to music for hours, or people who listen to their favorite albums on their commutes or while they jog every day, the people who listen to rhyming lyrics for wisdom have misplaced their inquiry.

The likelihood of anything poignant or quotable being committed to writing, and then also simultaneously rhyming, is incredibly low. That's because very little writing is poignant. The total number of poignant sentences typed by humanity, as a ratio to the total number of all sentences typed by humanity, is incredibly small. That's because most writing is expository, instructional or garbage.

Most of the writing you read day to day on the Internet is written by workman journalists, your friends, or freelance bloggers who write copy for click-bait content mills. The latter two groups compose the category of "garbage." Good journalists usually report only stories and news without interjecting much narrative or editorial, which doesn't lend itself to powerful or memorable prose. Then there's writing that is descriptive, which elucidates details of scenes, characters, or the world the writer lives in. So that leaves a handful of persuasive or narrative texts, and that's about it for all the quotable writing that humanity produces.

Most popular quotes are noteworthy precisely because they're pithy and rare. If most writing was quotable, powerful and concise enough to quote, people wouldn't quote anything. It'd be like that famous anecdote about one fish asking the other "How's the water?" and being answered "What the hell is water?" Only anomalies draw our attention, and quotable phrases are anomalies.

Then you have songwriters, poets and various free-form writers whose goal isn't necessarily to write powerful, quotable prose, but to write phrases that sound good when read out loud or sung to music. That's why if it rhymes, it's probably not important.

Take, for example, Shakespeare's famous quote "Brevity is the soul of wit." His saying is impactful because not only does the statement ring true, the sentence itself serves as an example of what it's professing to be true. If a songwriter were to write a similar phrase, he or she might be more concerned with rhymes, and the quote might be written as "Brevity is the soul of levity." Someone who heard it in a song might acclaim it for being witty, powerful, or poignant, when in fact it's stupid and meaningless— I can say this because I made it up randomly, just now.

Rhyming phrases that can even make sense are a symptom of a language with too many synonyms. The larger a writer's vocabulary, the more able they are to write rhymes in a showy display of their knowledge. Like all showy displays, it's rooted in insecurity. We get it, you know a lot of synonyms that end in similar sounds. Just because you can rhyme phrases together, doesn't mean you should. The purpose of writing is to communicate clearly, and rhyme makers concern themselves with the phonetic quality of their writing above everything else. Anything that impedes the fundamental goal of writing, which is incisiveness, necessarily makes it worse. Fuck rhymes.

FUCK ANTS

Ants just aren't impressive. Every time someone tells me an ant fact, my eyes glaze over from boredom and my heart rate flat lines. One of the most popular ant facts is that an ant can carry up to twenty times its weight. An ant weighs about five milligrams, so what's that, about an aspirin tablet? Big deal. I can carry a whole jar. Nothing about ants is impressive.

When people point out the vast number of ants, I'm not sure if it's an argument for or against the species. Since they are so plentiful, you'd think a few of them would have stood out by now—evolved the ability to bake a sheet of puff pastries or ride a bike. But no such ant exists. Ants have been around for 110–130 million years, so, evolutionarily speaking, they're a bust.

There are countless anecdotes and fables about ants, like those of Aesop, the ancient Greek storyteller. In his fable "The Ant and the Grasshopper," he writes about how ants are hard-working creatures who slave away all summer storing food for the winter, while the grasshopper—an alleged jackass—goofs around instead. When winter comes, the ants have plenty of food, and they mock the grasshopper mercilessly for not having any. The moral of the story is that ants are sociopaths. Imagine if humans gathered around for a giant feast and literally mocked another person for starving to death in the cold while they cheered and celebrated. That's an ant for you: the sadist of the arthropod phylum. Grasshoppers aren't equipped with digging mandibles in the first place, so blaming a grasshopper for not digging a hole to store food is like blaming a fish for not climbing a tree and cracking open a coconut. This fable doesn't even make sense on a basic level, because winter comes every year, and grasshoppers still seem to be around. That's because grasshoppers lay eggs that hatch when the weather gets warmer. How's that for planning ahead, dipshits? Not only do grasshoppers jerk around all summer and have fun, but also they don't even have to worry about survival through the winter because their progeny will emerge the following season ready to have fun again. Grasshoppers live the good life and peace-out just when shit gets cold. Ants worry and work year round just to wait out a blizzard in a literal dirt mound. Ants may survive the winter, but are they truly living? Ants are idiots.

When ants aren't mocking the homeless, they're busy dying. All ants do is work and die. Because the average ant's lifespan is about one year, every ant is a baby. Imagine if our planet was run by babies, and that's what you get with an ant society. When people claim that ants are social creatures, what they neglect to tell you is that ants are only social insofar as they're infants who can't do anything but move pebbles around. Even the matriarch, the ant queen, only lives at most ten or twenty years, not even old enough to buy alcohol in most countries. Not that it matters, because nobody wants to drink with someone carrying around a giant sack of pulsating larvae. Barf.

Ants communicate with pheromones they emit to signal to each other things like traces of food. If they detect any, they'll follow the scent like a fart trail to the source, like a butthole of sustenance, all the while stinking up the path behind them.

Stinging ants allegedly sting people only when they feel threatened, because of our size. But if that were the case, why do ants climb all over humans, seemingly without a care in the world? It'd be like a human feeling threatened by lava, then tempting fate by climbing around the edge of a volcano. If ants don't want to get killed by humans, here's an idea: Don't climb on us. Ants are egregious violators of personal space.

It's said that the weight of all the ants in the world accounts for approximately 25 percent of the weight of all animals and is equal in weight to the entire human race. Except instead of numbering roughly 7 billion, as humans do, ants number over 100 trillion. So that's approximately 14,285 ants per human. Seriously, do ants do anything other than fuck? Fuck ants.

FUCK YOUR OPINION
ON HUMANITY

The phrase "I've lost faith in humanity" has become ubiquitous. It's bandied about by millennials on social media any time they feel disappointed by life, which is always. Even if these self-appointed authorities did have a verifiable set of standards that humanity had unanimously agreed upon, they probably aren't qualified to have an opinion about it. In your twenty-three years of life, you probably haven't ruminated enough about the state of human affairs. You haven't experienced enough to have a meaningful opinion on humanity's ability to fulfill some arbitrary standard you have for it. What exactly is it that you have faith in humanity to do, and to what end? Faith is a trust or belief in something. Without stating what that faith is, it doesn't mean anything to say that you've lost it. That's kind of like running around saying "I'm disappointed." In what, dipshit? You can't just be disappointed. Without context, it doesn't mean anything.

If I had to guess what you had faith in humanity to do—and apparently I do have to guess, since you don't show the common courtesy of sharing your specific disappointment—it would be to accomplish some good. Or maybe more good than bad. But when people claim to "lose their faith," it's usually with regard to some story about an over-the-top food item, like a deep-fried donut sandwich. Or an offbeat story about a man stealing candy from a toddler. Even if we're to cede that these stories are examples of humanity faltering in its ability to produce some good, for a loss of faith in humanity to be justified there would have to be more examples of bad things occurring in the world than good to conclude that humanity is a lost cause.

There's usually no inquiry into the state of the world at the moment of the declaration. No survey of top news stories that day, weighed against all of the instances of good that humanity has produced in the same relative period. No consensus as to whether or not there has indeed been a shift in humanity and we have somehow regressed overnight into morons. There is no introspection or research, only an empty criticism, as if these critics were somehow above the group that comprises them. As if these stories that are so disheartening are the rule rather than the exception.

I don't care about your musings on life, shared from the air-conditioned comfort of your suburban home. Your traditional education, traditional employment and traditional family life haven't afforded you enough perspective on the humanity you're criticizing to critique it with any credibility. Not to mention historical perspective, since all of us have been alive for an amount of time that is statistically zero in the timeline of humanity. What exactly do you know about the daily condition of mankind that you didn't observe from movies, local news and trips to the grocery store? And how is your existence so bleak as to have completely lost faith, when survivors of war and genocide have so often been seen spreading messages of hope and redemption? Are you really so tortured and depressed by your life as to give up on not just it, but the lives of every other person on Earth? You saw a news story about someone doing something ridiculous or deplorable, so you think there is no further value in humans?

You know what? You're right. Humanity sucks. We have lost our capacity to produce good. Life is pretty rough, and there's no hope that it could ever get better. Why don't you take a leave of absence and spare yourself and, more important, us, from your tortured existence? I can think of few things worse than living in constant anguish, except for living next to it. Take your departure. Go somewhere else, where no one can disappoint you and your impossibly high standards for life.

That is, until you see a cute photo of a baby cuddling a piglet. Because now *that* calls for a social media post declaring a complete restoration of your faith in humanity. Thank God your faith in humanity was restored. We were all so worried about it. Your friends, family and work colleagues were all anxiously waiting since your last post for you to update them on your opinion of the state of the human race. Faith in humanity isn't a light switch for you to flip on and off, depending on which viral video you just watched. It's the condition of an advanced species, present company excluded.

FUCK YOU

You aren't that special. We're all taught to believe that we're precious little snowflakes and individuals in our own right, but most people shit, fuck, eat and sleep the same way. That's why there are scores of successful businesses that offer products and experiences that most people enjoy. They can predict what the masses will like based on what a few people like. As unique as we think we are, most people simply aren't. I am exceptional, of course, because I am the last collective hope of mankind, but that's another story.

The things that people think make them unique are looks, abilities, skills, talents, body types and personalities. But for every person who exists, with very few exceptions, there's someone who looks like you, has the same body type, similar abilities, skills, thoughts and talents. We delude ourselves into thinking that we're unique because we like seemingly obscure movies, books and genres of music. Well, get over yourself, Princess, lots of people like the things you like.

One particular source of pride people have in distinguishing themselves from the pack is their taste in music. I used to know someone who thought he was pretty esoteric for listening to live tapings of bands with no skill, following or potential. Then I wondered what space aliens would think of this smug idiot.

Would they be impressed by his laboriously unorthodox taste in "music" (Fig. 22)? Hell no, he'd be just another rectum to probe. Unless he had two rectums, he wouldn't even raise an extraterrestrial eyebrow. When we die, nobody will be able to recognize our sun-bleached skeletons from anyone else's.

Fig. 22: Aliens: not impressed by your musical taste.

Most humans have the same basic physiology. We all, for the most part, interpret light, sound, smell and taste the same way. That's why humans have so much food in common. The food of every major culture on Earth boils down to chicken and rice. The first time I tried Cuban food, I excitedly raved about it to my friends who hadn't tried it. They kept pressing me to describe it, and that's when I realized it is pretty much the same as Indian food, which is pretty much the same as Mediterranean food, which is pretty much the same as Chinese food. Japan has a different twist on it: fish and rice. And that's only if you ignore the popular Japanese dish of teriyaki chicken . . . and rice. Even Americans, both North and South, have chicken and rice dishes. We all eat the same food and turn it into shit, just the same.

This obsession with being unique probably comes from stories, fairy tales, movies and other entertainment that focuses on protagonists. They are distinct from other people in that we focus on them. Their individual stories make them seem like individuals. Take, for example, the classic fairy tale of Robin Hood. He's a pretty interesting character when we dissect the moral complexity and contradictions that make him who he is. But if you imagine a scene in which Robin Hood was hatching a plot to rob a rich aristocrat and redistribute his wealth, and then pictured that scene from several thousand miles away, you'd realize he was just an insignificant dot doing nothing of consequence. Even major historical events in our timeline are trivial in the grand scheme of the universe. We only think we're significant because we keep a written record of our relatively recent history. The billions of chickens killed annually to serve alongside rice have no such biographical record. Do their individual lives matter? I would contend not, and neither do ours. Everything is either chicken and rice, or composed of chicken and rice. *You* are chicken and rice.

When more than 100 billion humans have lived, chances are pretty low that there's anything special about you. Even our historical figures, like Napoleon, Alexander the Great, or King Tutankhamen, had distinctions bestowed upon them by society, not any superhuman authority. An analysis of Tutankhamen's mummified remains, for example, revealed that he was a frail nineteen-year-old boy who had crippling genetic disabilities due to incest,[94] and he likely died from complications due to malaria—a disease that kills over half a million people each year. Yeah, real special.

The strength, bravery, diligence, wealth, or status some people enjoy, while uncommon, aren't unique. Show me a person who can breathe underwater, and then historians might give a shit about how special you are. In fact, people are so similar that even discovering a person who could breathe underwater would give the person who discovered him or her special distinction as a "discoverer." We're all so unimportant and similar that even the first *observation* of the unusual gives us celebrated status in historical texts.

Despite the diversity that exists in the bird kingdom, all birds have enough traits in common for them to be classified together, and birds are far more unique than humans. Some birds fly, some are landlubbers and some can swim. Some eat only fish, while others eat fruit and worms and still others eat mammals. And unlike humans, birds are this way out of physiological and evolutionary necessity, not the need to be a pretentious pain in the ass when you go out to a restaurant. Your gluten sensitivity and "pescetarian" identity don't make you unique, beyond uniquely annoying.

Your parents, teachers and entertainment icons have been lying to you: You're not unique or special. Nobody will be able to recognize your corpse in a mass grave. This is never more obvious than when one observes . . . a mass grave. These exist in the catacombs in France, and they are available to visit whenever you need a stark reminder of how ordinary you are.

Say you were to become the richest person in the world. Do you think the aforementioned aliens would give a shit? If you were abducted along with a homeless person, stripped of clothing and set on a probing table, would your extraterrestrial overlords care that your bank account has X number of dollars in it? Only as much as you care which squirrel has the most acorns stashed away.

If your distinction involves something you can do on Earth, chances are that lots of people have done it. Climbing the world's tallest mountain or plumbing the world's deepest depth is still just a numeric distinction. If you had to make a case for your uniqueness, simply having a number that represents a vertical distance you traveled up or down isn't going to impress anyone processing humans for food. You will have failed to be unique, just like you will have failed at everything else in life, except for being nutritious.

Fuck you.

ACKNOWLEDGMENTS

First and foremost, a big fuck you to everyone who didn't think I'd finish this book. There were many. You're all wrong. Fuck you.

Next, I'd like to thank Jessica Blum for her kindness, support and encouragement. For someone whose name isn't on the cover of this book, she was with me on far too many 3 a.m. coffee sprints.

Thank you to Taylor Nikolai and Sarah Peretz who helped me make a breakthrough when I was stuck in a quagmire of aimless brilliance. Their guidance, support and suggestions helped give this manuscript direction and steered me back on track. This book wouldn't be the same without them.

Big thanks to Michael Malice for his advice, encouragement and support. Michael gave input on countless insane book covers that were pitched, and helped settle on one that was equal parts classy and crass. Michael's insight has been invaluable to me over the years, not only on this book but also my previous published works. And on that note, thanks to my good friends Marie and Roger Barr, who helped come up with many of the aforementioned insane covers. You guys are a wellspring of creativity, talent and kindness. Thanks to Justin Killion for being there for me and for the years of friendship and support—and for finally bringing my vision to the screen.

A huge thanks to Jeremie Ruby-Strauss who has been consistently badass since we first started working together in 2004. Jeremie is a very reasonable man in a very unreasonable world. Thanks to Nina Cordes for doing an excellent job coordinating literally everything.

Thanks to Brian Cooperman and Lauren Alexandra Lewis for their tireless support and late-night Korean BBQ brainstorming sessions. Their friendship and support are invaluable. Thanks to my homey Rucka Rucka Ali who will never read this book or even realize I thanked him and gave him a promotion. Thanks to Mikey Bolts for his support and being such a badass. Thanks to Cherry and Jay for their tireless support and kindness; you are truly top-shelf people.

Thanks to Leah Tiscione for her support and encouragement; she was there in the trenches with me when I first started writing this manuscript. Friends of her caliber and talent don't come along often, and I'm proud to call her my friend. Speaking of, thanks to Brad Webb and his beer-fueled but brilliant late-night ideas. FCTC. Thanks to Laurie and Erek Foster, who are two of the most badass people I've ever met. They're not only crazy talented but they also possess integrity in an era bereft of it. Thanks to Dan Berman for his inspiration, support and brilliant caffeine-fueled inspiration at 3 a.m. during our countless all-nighters.

Thanks to Jessica Safron, Louis Fernet-Leclair, Joe, Jamye, Justin, Nort, Cheryl, Bryce, Ellie, Mike Gamms, Chad, Mack, Caitlin, Shawn Schepps, David, Eleni, Leopold, Samurai Dan K, Sargon, Genevieve and Jesse. Thanks to my parents for all that they did right and wrong to inadvertently help produce this angry tome. Thanks to Dino and crew at Stir Crazy for keeping the coffee pouring during countless ten-hour marathon sessions. Thanks to Alex Berg, Deborah, Wayland, Soike, Fernie, Amber, the brilliant Lord Matthew, Iffy, Haley, Gina, Tim Chang, Tim Baker and all my friends who came through for me. Thank you, Ela Darling, you are amazing and may people wear your Dewey decimal some day.

And finally, thanks to Austin Blank for absolutely nothing.

NOTES

1. https://www.scientificamerican.com/article/packaged-whale-meat-in-ja/.

2. http://www.sciencefocus.com/qa/how-many-trees-are-needed-provide-enough-oxygen-one-person.

3. http://www.businessinsider.com/comparing-genetic-similarity-between-humans-and-other-things-2016-5/#a-2005-study-found-that-chimpanzees-our-closest-living-evolutionary-relatives-are-96-genetically-similar-to-humans-2.

4. https://d21.org/wp-content/uploads/2017/01/Statistics_2_Perpetrators.pdf.

5. https://www.theguardian.com/books/2015/may/29/game-of-thrones-war-of-roses-hbo.

6. http://www.bu.edu/history/files/2015/09/245fall15.pdf.

7. Nancy Lewis Tuten and John Zubizarreta, *The Robert Frost Encyclopedia* (Westport, CT: Greenwood Publishing Group, 2000), 230–31.

8. Edward Connery Lathem and Lawrance Thompson, eds., *The Robert Frost Reader* (New York: Macmillan, 2002), 106.

9. Tuten and Zubizarreta, *Robert Frost Encyclopedia*, 349.

10. http://www.modernamericanpoetry.org/criticism/richard-poirier-stopping-woods-snowy-evening.

11. Tuten and Zubizarreta, *Robert Frost Encyclopedia*, 349.

12. https://www.washingtonpost.com/news/parenting/wp/2016/01/07/matilda-and-the-challenge-of-deciding-whats-appropriate-for-kids-at-what-age/.

13. Margaret L Andersen and Howard F. Taylor, *Sociology: Understanding a Diverse Society*, 4th ed. (Belmont, CA: Thomson Learning, 2008), 146.

14. http://www.livescience.com/40858-tail-wag-direction-dog-behavior.html.

15. https://www.nytimes.com/2015/02/15/magazine/how-one-stupid-tweet-ruined-justine-saccos-life.html.

16. https://www.whitehouse.gov/the-press-office/2014/04/08/executive-order-non-retaliation-disclosure-compensation-information.

17. https://www.rainn.org/images/03-2014/WH-Task-Force-RAINN-Recommendations.pdf.

18. https://www.thenation.com/article/ten-things-end-rape-culture/.

19. http://theweek.com/speedreads/545010/dolce-gabbana-backtrack-homophobic-comments-maybe-chose-wrong-words.

20. http://www.reprolife.net/news/how-gabbana-asked-a-female-friend-to-have-a-baby-for-him-years-before-dandg-storm-over-branding-elton-johns-kids-synthetic.

21. http://www.telegraph.co.uk/news/celebritynews/11473198/Sir-Elton-John-calls-for-Dolce-and-Gabbana-boycott-after-row-over-same-sex-families.html.

22. http://news.bbc.co.uk/onthisday/hi/dates/stories/july/25/newsid_2499000/2499411.stm.

23. http://www2.census.gov/prod2/statcomp/documents/CT1970p2-13.pdf.

24. https://www.theguardian.com/world/2016/mar/07/north-korea-threatens-to-reduce-us-and-south-korea-to-flames-and-ash.

25. https://www.ksl.com/?sid=34628265.

26. http://kfor.com/2014/12/12/proposed-satanic-statue-being-created-ten-commandments-to-be-rebuilt/.

27. http://newsok.com/article/5485152.

28. http://www.usatoday.com/story/news/2015/10/06/after-court-order-10-commandments-monument-is-removed-from-grounds-of-oklahoma-state-capitol/73445134/.

29. https://www.washingtonpost.com/news/the-intersect/wp/2016/07/21/what-it-takes-to-get-banned-from-twitter/.

30. http://www.washingtontimes.com/news/2016/jul/20/milo-yiannopoulos-twitter-ban-reignites-accusation/.

31. http://www.theharrispoll.com/health-and-life/Censorship_2015.html.

32. http://clas.mq.edu.au/speech/infinite_sentences/.

33. http://booksearch.blogspot.com/2010/08/books-of-world-stand-up-and-be-counted.html.

34. https://strainindex.wordpress.com/2008/07/28/the-average-sentence-length/.

35. http://www.edmondschools.net/Portals/3/docs/Terri_McGill/READ
    -Bystander%20effect.pdf.

36. http://www.alsa.org/news/media/press-releases/ice-bucket-challenge-082914.
    html.

37. http://www.vox.com/2014/8/20/6040435/als-ice-bucket-challenge-and-why
    -we-give-to-charity-donate.

38. http://newsfeed.time.com/2013/03/26/what-is-the-red-equal-sign-all-over
    -facebook-and-twitter/.

39. http://www.theguardian.com/sustainable-business/likes-dont-save-lives
    -unicef-social-media.

40. https://www.youtube.com/watch?v=2_M0SDk3ZaM.

41. http://www.news.com.au/world/remember-kony-2012-well-its-2013-what
    -happened/story-fndir2ev-1226550575923.

42. http://www.guidestar.org/FinDocuments/2011/542/164/2011-542164338
    -07bf621f-9.pdf.

43. http://www.state.gov/j/ct/rls/other/des/123086.htm.

44. http://www.state.gov/r/pa/prs/ps/2012/03/186734.htm.

45. http://www.independent.co.ug/column/insight/1039-revisiting-operation
    -lightning-thunder-.

46. https://www.whitehouse.gov/the-press-office/statement-president-signing
    -lords-resistance-army-disarmament-and-northern-uganda-r.

47. http://content.usatoday.com/communities/theoval/post/2011/10/obama
    -dispatches-100-troops-to-uganda/1.

48. http://www.upi.com/blog/2013/04/03/5-million-bounty-offered-for-Joseph
    -Kony/2981365016264/.

49. http://www.ubos.org/UNHS0910/chapter7.Average%20Monthly%20
    Household%20Income.html.

50. http://www.itu.int/en/ITU-D/Statistics/Documents/statistics/2015/Fixed
    _broadband_2000-2014.xls.

51. http://www.theguardian.com/world/2012/mar/14/kony-2012-screening
    -anger-northern-uganda.

52. http://www.monitor.co.ug/News/National/-/688334/1387926/-/aw2cd3z/-/
    index.html.

53. http://blogs.aljazeera.com/blog/africa/ugandans-react-anger-kony-video.

54. http://www.independent.co.uk/news/world/africa/lra-war-crimes-trial
    -joseph-kony-general-abducted-into-lords-resistance-army-as-a-child-is
    -charged-10004053.html.

55. http://news.bbc.co.uk/2/hi/africa/7926173.stm.

56. http://haas.berkeley.edu/faculty/papers/anderson/status%20enhancement%20 account%20of%20overconfidence.pdf.

57. https://www.nytimes.com/2016/10/13/us/why-last-second-lane-mergers-are -good-for-traffic.html.

58. Alan Axelrod, *Patton: A Biography* (New York: Palgrave Macmillan, 2006), 118.

59. http://usda.mannlib.cornell.edu/usda/nass/LiveSlau//2010s/2015/ LiveSlau-01-22-2015.txt.

60. http://www.ers.usda.gov/topics/animal-products/poultry-eggs/statistics -information.aspx.

61. http://usda.mannlib.cornell.edu/usda/nass/LiveSlau//2010s/2015/ LiveSlau-06-25-2015.txt.

62. http://usda.mannlib.cornell.edu/usda/nass/LiveSlau//2010s/2015/ LiveSlau-07-23-2015.txt.

63. http://www.vegetariantimes.com/article/vegetarianism-in-america/.

64. Christian J. Peters, Jamie Picardy, Amelia F. Darrouzet-Nardi, Jennifer L. Wilkins, Timothy S. Griffin, and Gary W. Fick, "Carrying capacity of U.S. agricultural land: Ten diet scenarios." *Elementa: Science of the Anthropocene* 4 (2016): 116, http://doi.org/10.12952/journal.elementa.000116.

65. http://www.vrg.org/journal/vj98jan/981coord.htm.

66. Peter Singer, *Animal Liberation: The Definitive Classic of the Animal Movement*, 40th anniversary ed. (New York: Open Road Media, 2015), 244.

67. Daniel Chamovitz, *What a Plant Knows: A Field Guide to the Senses* (New York: Scientific American / Farrar, Straus and Giroux, 2012), 8.

68. Chamovitz, *What a Plant Knows*, 82.

69. S. Leonard Bastin, *Can a Plant Feel Pain?*, *Scientific American* 109, July 1913, 186. https://babel.hathitrust.org/cgi/pt?id=pst.000063000085;view=1up;seq= 190.

70. http://www.nature.com/scitable/knowledge/library/plant-resistance-against -herbivory-96675700.

71. http://theconversation.com/ordering-the-vegetarian-meal-theres-more -animal-blood-on-your-hands-4659.

72. http://plato.stanford.edu/entries/turing-test/.

73. http://www.smashingmagazine.com/2011/03/in-search-of-the-perfect -captcha/.

74. http://www.bbc.co.uk/blogs/bbcinternet/2010/10/captcha_and_bbc_id.html.

75. https://moz.com/blog/captchas-affect-on-conversion-rates.

76. http://www.bbc.com/news/technology-24710209.

77. http://web.stanford.edu/~jurafsky/burszstein_2010_captcha.pdf.

78. https://news.vice.com/article/drone-footage-shows-extent-of-damage-from-greenpeace-stunt-at-nazca-lines.

79. http://whc.unesco.org/en/list/700.

80. http://www.universetoday.com/12648/will-earth-survive-when-the-sun-becomes-a-red-giant/.

81. http://www.bbc.com/earth/story/20150323-how-long-will-life-on-earth-last.

82. http://gizmodo.com/apollo-11s-source-code-is-a-surprisingly-hilarious-arti-1783415335.

83. http://www.apa.org/topics/divorce/.

84. http://classics.mit.edu/Plato/symposium.html.

85. http://www.lightningsafety.noaa.gov/fatalities.shtml.

86. http://mentalfloss.com/article/58235/11-mundane-objects-are-statistically-deadlier-sharks.

87. http://news.rutgers.edu/research-news/sniffing-out-danger-rutgers-scientists-say-fearful-memories-can-trigger-heightened-sense-smell/20131212#.VcmkMflViko.

88. https://web.archive.org/web/20131122144749/http://new.oberlin.edu/office/equity-concerns/sexual-offense-resource-guide/prevention-support-education/support-resources-for-faculty.dot.

89. Matthew Bernstein, *Controlling Hollywood: Censorship and Regulation in the Studio Era* (New Brunswick, NJ: Rutgers University Press,1999), 1.

90. http://www.ala.org/advocacy/intfreedom/librarybill/interpretations/labelingrating.

91. http://www.ala.org/advocacy/intfreedom/librarybill/interpretations/qa-labeling.

92. http://www.aaup.org/report/trigger-warnings.

93. https://www.as.ucsb.edu/senate/resolutions/a-resolution-to-mandate-warnings-for-triggering-content-in-academic-settings/.

94. http://www.scientificamerican.com/article/king-tut-dna/.

ILLUSTRATION CREDITS

Fig. 1: https://pixabay.com/en/sperm-whale-beached-dead-ocean-904349/

Fig. 2: https://en.wikipedia.org/wiki/File:Feeding_Priscilla.jpg

Pg. 5: Louis Fernet-Leclair

Fig. 3: https://commons.wikimedia.org/wiki/File:Beluga_Whale_Vancouver_Aquarium.JPG (Ubergirl) Photo modified and heading added.

Fig. 4: https://pixabay.com/en/pool-table-billiards-rack-balls-16723/

Fig. 5: https://pixabay.com/en/pub-horsebar-old-western-hat-1073945/

Fig. 6: https://pixabay.com/en/skull-death-horse-teeth-anatomy-646628/

Fig. 7: https://commons.wikimedia.org/wiki/File:The_horse_and_its_relatives_BHL21572638.jpg

Fig. 8: https://commons.wikimedia.org/wiki/File:CamelSkelLyd2.png

Fig. 9: https://en.wikipedia.org/wiki/Road_signs_in_Finland/

Fig. 10: Created by Author

Fig. 11: Photo courtesy of the German Federal Archive: https://commons.wikimedia.org/wiki/File:Bundesarchiv_B_145_Bild-F051673-0059,_Adolf_Hitler_und_Eva_Braun_auf_dem_Berghof.jpg

Fig. 12: Jessica Safron

Fig. 13: Jessica Safron

Fig. 14: Jessica Safron

Fig. 15: Photograph by Andrew Bossi (https://commons.wikimedia.org/wiki/File:4377_-_Bern_-_Kindlifresserbrunnen_am_Kornhausplatz.JPG)

Fig. 16: https://pixabay.com/en/fairy-tower-landscape-cappadocia-765501/

Fig. 17: Source—Google Trends search for "the war on terror"

Fig. 18: Source—Google Trends search for "rape culture"

Fig. 19: http://www.telegraph.co.uk/technology/facebook/10041713/Likes-dont-save-lives-charity-hits-out-at-Facebook-slacktivists.html

Fig. 20: Jessica Safron

Fig. 21: Jessica Safron

Fig. 22: Jessica Safron

FOLLOW MADDOX

Twitter: @maddoxrules
Instagram: @realmaddox
Facebook: facebook.com/maddoxrules
Website: http://maddox.xmission.com